Dating, Relationships, and Sexuality

What Teens Should Know

ISSUES IN FOCUS TODAY

Wendy Hart Beckman

Enslow Publishers, Inc.
40 Industrial Road
Box 398
Berkeley Heights, NJ 07922
USA

http://www.enslow.com

Library of Congress Cataloging-in-Publication Data

Beckman, Wendy Hart.
    Dating, relationships, and sexuality : what teens should know / Wendy Hart
Beckman.
        p. cm. — (Issues in focus today)
    Includes bibliographical references and index.
    ISBN 0-7660-1948-9
    1. Dating (Social customs)—Juvenile literature. 2. Interpersonal relations in
adolescence—Juvenile literature. 3. Sexual ethics for teenagers—Juvenile literature.
4. Adolescent psychology—Juvenile literature. I. Title. II. Series.
    HQ801.B363   2006
    306.730835—dc22

                                                                    2005033726

Printed in the United States of America

10 9 8 7 6 5 4 3 2 1

To Our Readers:
We have done our best to make sure that all Internet addresses in this book were active and
appropriate when we went to press. However, the author and publisher have no control
over and assume no liability for the material available on those Internet sites or on other
Web sites they may link to. Any comments or suggestions can be sent by e-mail to com-
ments@enslow.com or to the address on the back cover.

Illustration Credits: AP/Wide World, pp. 35, 99; BananaStock, pp. 3, 14, 74, 78, 101, 103;
Corbis Images Royalty-Free, pp. 3, 17, 21, 47, 93; Corel Corp., p. 39; Digital Vision,
pp. 3, 5, 32, 85, 105; EyeWire Images, p. 54; Library of Congress, pp. 3, 50, 58;
Photos.com, pp. 1, 3, 8, 11, 27, 29, 42, 61, 65, 69, 82, 87, 97.

Cover Illustration: Corbis Images Royalty-Free (large illustration); BananaStock (small
illustration).

Contents

Acknowledgments

I would like to thank the many teenagers and parents who contributed to this work. So that I may respect their privacy, I cannot acknowledge them by name. You know who you are; please know also that I respect your openness and willingness to share your stories with others. (Names that have been changed are in quotation marks.)

I also want to thank Mary Smith for her insight gained from many, many years teaching sixth graders and her enthusiastic research on my behalf. Her adoration from her former pupils is well earned.

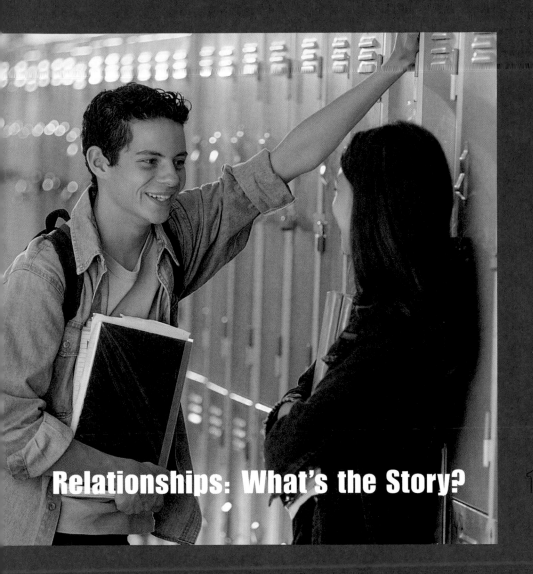

Relationships: What's the Story?

Fifteen-year-old LaRon went with "Angela" for one day. He was asked, "Did you really go *out* or just announce it?" He answered, "Oh, we announced it. I don't want that girl eatin' outta *my* popcorn!"[1]

Not all teens may have the same attitude toward dating as LaRon does, but all have questions and concerns over forming and making decisions about relationships. As we enter the twenty-first century, it is clear that teenagers continue to face challenges and choices that teens of the past have faced. It is also clear that modern teens are entering into relationships that people of even fifty years ago could not have imagined. Who would have thought a person could go out, go steady, and break up with another person—without ever leaving his or her own home? This situation is not only possible, but common—thanks to the advent of the Internet, cell phones, and instant messaging (IM). Not only do teenagers have more choices, but they also *hear* more about those choices. The Internet, e-mail, instant messaging, and cable television have vastly expanded our knowledge and perceptions. Sometimes the media raise more questions than they answer. Mass media have also increased our fears and doubts.

This book is an attempt to dispel some fears, disprove some myths, and dispense some information about relationships, dating, and sex for teenagers. The intent is to inform, not preach; to document, not generalize; and to answer as many questions as possible—and perhaps generate new ones for teens to answer for themselves. Throughout these pages, many topics will be examined: controversial subjects, health issues, dating customs, and cultural differences.

> **Today's teenagers continue to face challenges and choices that teens of the past have faced; they are also entering into relationships that people of even fifty years ago could never have imagined.**

Dating rituals have changed over the years, along with fashions, public tolerance, and society's standards. Teenagers face some of the same problems that their parents and grandparents did: wondering about their own self-worth, trying to fit in with their desired peer groups, and making efforts to attract and retain a significant other. However, as previously noted and as most teens know, twenty-first century teens differ from the teens of the early twentieth century, such as in the ways that they communicate and form relationships.

It is also important to note that just as today's teens are different from their grandparents, they are also different from one another, with special concerns. Many times teenagers are banded together under one description, says Sarah Heath, a history professor at Texas A&M University in Corpus Christi. Heath has studied teenagers throughout recent history. She says that teens are often painted with one "broad brush," as if they all acted the same. But knowing the behavior of one teenager does not predict the behavior of another.

Nevertheless, there are trends that can be described in general terms. As with any attempt to look at a large group of people, many individuals will not fit the general description or stereotype. (People *outside* the group will even fit some characteristics.) On the other hand, there will be people in the group who fit the group's description to a *T*.

"I would argue it is dangerous to 'lump' youth together into a homogenous blob and to assume they all act the same in any time period," says Heath. "Class, race, belief systems, and even popular culture influence young people as much as do their peers and each young person responds in distinct ways."[2]

Communication Overload

One way in which teenagers today *are* alike is that they face an overabundance of communication. Information is easily available through the broadcast media, such as television and radio, as well as interactive media, such as the Internet. That "easily available" communication, however, means that more people than ever also have access *to* those same teens. In that way, teenagers are more vulnerable than ever to misinformation. The "information highway" has tremendous opportunities, but it also has wrong turns and unclear signs.

When it comes to dating and sex, teenagers are often given the benefit of their parents' opinions and advice. Parents are legally and morally responsible for their teenage children, of course. Beyond that, however, parents have the advantage of having been teenagers once themselves. They also know their own teenagers from a historical perspective. That is, they knew their teenagers as children. However, they might not be familiar with the young adults that their children are becoming. Many teenagers might not themselves recognize the person they are becoming, either. Both the teens and their parents have to feel their way through the new relationship and play a few things by ear.

Parents might remember their own relationships from the past: boy meets girl; boy asks girl out; girl says yes or no. Was it ever that simple? In the United States until recently, males were expected to ask females out. This pattern is changing in two ways: More girls are asking boys out, and many boys and girls

When it comes to relationships, many things are different for today's teens than they were for their parents. But they can still learn from each other.

are asking out people of their own gender. Teens are challenged in identifying their sexual orientation and gender identity. How do teens initiate relationships with others who are also struggling with their own sexuality?

How Dating Works Today—Or Doesn't

Sometimes the seeds for romantic "success" or "failure" are sown in relationships with friends and family members. There are basic steps that take place in all dating relationships: The couple meets; the two people get to know each other on some level; they become romantically involved. These steps can take hours or years from start to finish. Do relationships that take longer to develop last longer? Not always. Some dating relationships started out as friendships. For some, the attraction was always there and so the relationship was approached as a romantic one, rather than as a friendship, in the first place.

Another variety of romantic relationship is dating without sexual activity. The relationship at this point can lead to future commitment, including engagement and marriage, before any sexual activity occurs. Finally, the last broad possibility for the romantic category includes sexual involvement.

Many teens are getting sexually involved, with or without protection or preparation. The risks of unprotected sexual intercourse include pregnancy and disease. According to the American College of Osteopathic Family Physicians (ACOFP), although teen birthrates in the United States are falling, more teenagers in the United States are having babies than teenagers in most other industrialized countries.[3] While teenage pregnancy is down in the United States, the level of sexually transmitted diseases continues to rise.

Most adults recognize that, as teenagers, they rushed into some actions without thinking them through. Teenagers experience more freedom than they did as children. With that freedom comes the responsibility of having to make decisions without parents around to give hints at what the "right" decision is (or at least what they think the right decision is). One of those decisions is whether to get sexually involved with another person.

Referring to sexual involvement as a decision is not very romantic. That is one reason why teenagers need to seek information ahead of time—so that they have a feeling what the right decision is for them when the time comes. If their decision is to become sexually active, then the next decision is what kind of risks and preparation are involved.

One way to look at sexual involvement is that the teen years are a time to "try on" different relationships and not get committed to one long-term one. Sometimes when people get sexually involved too soon, they take away their own freedom to make other choices. Teens grow and change, and their relationship needs change, too.

When seeking information, we should never rely on just one source for that information. We should look for guidance from credible sources and then balance that external information with our own self-knowledge. Like any other single source of information, this book should not dictate what all teenagers should do or should not do. Instead, the trends from the past are presented so that those lessons can be applied to the future. Think of it as a road atlas, allowing for a variety of experiences, but always aiming to ensure a safe and pleasant journey. Bon voyage!

Communication

Morgan (15), by IM: *Talk and talk and talk and talk some more but let the other person get some words in also . . . call ppl and if u like su1 let them kno . . . and when u talk dont tell lies 2 make urself look better because they always get thrown at u.*[1]

Developing relationships hinges on many skills. Communication is probably the most important of those skills.

Generally, males and females do not communicate in the same ways. Most boys communicate in a way that is acceptable to their friends' version of masculinity. They seldom discuss emotions with other boys. To admit to feelings is like admitting to being weak. Boys risk having other boys laugh at them or ridicule them for weakness. When boys talk about feelings, it is usually with a girl—but not necessarily a girlfriend.[2]

Many boys do not know how to connect with girls. Drs. Dan Kindlon and Michael Thompson wrote *Raising Cain: Protecting the Emotional Life of Boys.* "Most have so little grounding in emotional communication that they can't even imagine what intimacy is," they say.

> They've had few lessons in learning to "read" others, to pick up on emotional cues through conversation, facial expression, or other subtle body language. It is hard to be empathic when you can't understand what someone else is feeling, and because boys have not been encouraged to cultivate empathy, they misread social and sexual cues from girls: they can't figure out what a girl might think or want.[3]

Males tend to build hierarchies. Much communication is aimed at establishing order. Females, on the other hand, tend to build relationships. Communication is aimed at sharing personal experiences and finding common ground.

"For girls, talk is the glue that holds relationships together," says sociolinguist Deborah Tannen. "Boys' relationships are held together primarily by activities: doing things together, or talking about activities such as sports or, later, politics."[4] For this reason, both boys and girls can be frustrated when a member of the other gender is talking.

Electronic Communication

More than a hundred years ago, most personal communication took place face-to-face or by letter. After 1876, some communication occurred by telephone, thanks to Alexander Graham Bell. Just a little more than a century later, in 2000, 98 percent of U.S. households had telephone service, according to the U.S. Census.[5]

But adults in households fortunate enough to be in the telephone-owning majority often find it hard to get any time on the phone. Even back in the 1950s and 1960s, teenagers began spending hours on the phone. Some teenagers in the 1960s and 1970s began getting their own telephones, often as an extension off the main line. Parents set time limits for when their teenagers had to get off the phone. Electronics had hit teenage communications.

Then the personal computer came along. In the 1970s, only organizations like the government, businesses, or colleges had computers. By the mid-1980s, households began owning PCs—personal computers. Not surprisingly, the generation that was born in the age of the personal computer relies on it for communicating. America Online (AOL) conducted a study of Internet use by teenagers. AOL found that 81 percent of teenagers from ages twelve to seventeen use the Internet for e-mailing friends and relatives. Of 6,700 teenagers and their parents surveyed, 70 percent used the Internet for instant messaging from their computers. Of teens in the study aged eighteen and nineteen, 91 percent used e-mail and 83 percent used IM; 56 percent liked using the Internet more than the telephone.[6]

Much communication among boys is built around establishing order, while much communication among girls is aimed at building relationships.

The Pew Internet and American Life Project, in which both adults and youths were asked questions about their lifestyles, was conducted in 2000. In the project, 754 teenagers were asked about their Internet use. Of them, 74 percent said that they used IM. And most of the teenagers who used IM did so more than they relied on e-mails.[7]

Instant messaging by computer and text messaging by cell phone have the immediacy of conversations held face-to-face or by telephone. However, it is one step removed from talking in person. The sender and the receiver are reading their conversation. They cannot see or hear the other person. This "distance" has both advantages and disadvantages. In the Pew study, 37 percent of the teens said that they could IM things they would never say in person. Also, 17 percent of the teens said that they had used IM to ask someone out for a first date. Even breakups come more easily now. In the Pew study, 13 percent of

Since men and women tend to have different communication styles, sometimes it can be difficult for them to understand each other.

the teenagers said that they had broken up with someone through IM.[8]

Another advantage/disadvantage to electronic communication is the cloak of secrecy we can put on. Besides hiding aspects of our personality, as discussed earlier, we can also hide our identity. Almost one quarter of the teenagers in the Pew study said that they had a secret screen name so their friends would not know that they were online. An equal number said that they had pretended they were someone else while IMing. They've dished it out and they've had to take it, too. One third of the teens reported that they had been given false information while instant messaging.[9]

Dr. Amy Bowles Reyer is the author of *Our Secret Garden: Sex Education in Teen Fiction for Girls in the 1970s.* She has a Ph.D. in American Studies from George Washington University and is the host and producer of a television show called *The Women's Club With Amy Reyer.* Dr. Reyer concluded that a big trend for what she calls "Generation IM," is that teenagers are spending less time *truly* alone, reading, or listening to music (for example).

Historian Sarah Heath says:

> I wonder what impact computer use has had on relationships. My students seem to be as comfortable flirting at online chat services or by text message as they [are gathering] in larger "real time" social groups. To be sure, many people still form families, and young people still seem to believe that they eventually will commit to a long-term relationship—but how they go about finding their mates and spending social time has changed.[10]

American teenagers are not unusual in relying on electronic media for communication. Euro RSCG Worldwide is the world's fifth-largest marketing, advertising, and communications agency. Euro RSCG studied teenagers' online behavior in Australia and around the world. They conducted a study, "Connected and Connectivity—The Power of Teens Online," to look at teens' attitudes and lifestyles. Their results showed that American and Australian teenagers had a lot in common. More than three fourths of American teenagers ages thirteen to eighteen accessed the Internet at least once a week. Similarly, 75 percent of Australian teenagers were online at least weekly.[11] These numbers are similar to those for Great Britain's teenagers. Japan, Korea, and Sweden were the only countries where teenagers accessed the Internet more often than American teens. Teens in the study said that they realized that they tended to rely on the Internet too much instead of live face-to-face interactions.[12]

"Generation Y"—those born in the 1980s and 1990s—will see fewer distinctions between countries than earlier generations did. As with telephone conversations, however, Internet chats and IM will depend on people being awake at the same time. At least with "old-fashioned" e-mails, people can wait until their own time is right for corresponding. Perhaps time-zone boundaries will someday become more important than country borders.

Popularity and Body Image

3

The word *popular* comes from a Latin word meaning "of the people." We use it to mean being liked by a lot of people. Is it necessary to be popular to develop a relationship? No. Quality, not quantity, matters most in developing a relationship. First, you need to like yourself. Teenagers, as with people of all ages, need to respect themselves if they want or expect others to respect them.

R-E-S-P-E-C-T ... Y-O-U-R-S-E-L-F

Stedman Graham is a marketing consultant, an adjunct instructor at the University of Chicago and the University of Illinois at

Chicago, and a visiting professor at Coker College in Hartsville, South Carolina. As the author of *Teens Can Make It Happen*, Graham often speaks to large audiences about the pressures that young people face and how young people can achieve success. In his book *Move Without the Ball: Put Your Skills and Your Magic to Work for You!*, Graham says:

> When your self-identity and self-esteem are strong, when you are confident and assured in your abilities and in your essential value as a human being, when you have respect for yourself and for others, the more likely you are to make good daily choices. You aren't in control of everything that happens to you, but you are in control of how you respond to life and of the choices you make.[1]

Teens in this group interview make a similar point to Graham's:

> LaRon (15): *"Everybody likes me. I've got skills. I'm athletic. . . . Popularity is about being who you are."*
> Mark (14): *"People will like you if you act the way you want to and don't be self-conscious."*
> Chris (12): *"It kind of works for me. I try to be myself."*
> Mark: *"Sometimes things you can't control affect your popularity, like if you have braces or funny teeth or big frizzy nasty hair or if you were born with a speech impediment or something like that. Stuff like that affects your popularity."*[2]

How pleased are teenagers with their bodies? As our society has placed more emphasis upon finding the perfect physique, individuals often think about how their own bodies measure up.

Desirability Yesterday and Today

Before the invasion of mass media, when people were more locally limited, people had only the others around them to look at. Potential spouses were evaluated on the basis of how good their bloodlines were. That is, did their older family members live to healthy, ripe old ages, or did they all tend to die too young after spending most of their lives being ill? The best choices for future mates—personally and for the species—were those who were survivors. Their appearance and their family history implied that they would live a long life and be a good parent to their many healthy children.

Then, as high fashion developed over the centuries, women and men started looking at people less as future parents to their children and more in an almost artistic sense. Media, such as newspapers, magazines, television, and (recently) the Internet, showed images of both men and women as works of art to evaluate and to admire. Also, many people have made a conscious choice to avoid parenthood. This might negate the formerly subconscious criterion of whether someone would make a good mother or father.

Body Size and Self-Worth

> Mark: *"It's amazing how some people can overcome their body size by their attitude. 'Ethan' is the most popular kid, but he's huge, dude! It's easier for boys. Big girls can't overcome their size that easy. Society accepts overweight boys more than they do girls."*[3]

Up until the beginning of the twentieth century, an overweight person was considered to be healthy. Extra weight was also a sign of higher status. It meant that a person was financially comfortable enough to buy plenty of food and did not have to engage in manual labor for a living.

Then in the early 1900s, as women began being more active in business as well as physical leisure activities, they found that the Victorian-era plumpness was a disadvantage. Whether by intention or just happenstance, women began to mold themselves after a less weighty ideal than had previous generations. Excess weight was seen as a sign of laziness and self-indulgence. The ideal woman of the early 1900s was five feet four inches tall and weighed 140 pounds.[4] In the 1920s, the flapper image encouraged women to look even thinner and flatter—almost boyish.

What was considered ideal in women's figures changed throughout the decades of the twentieth century. To many, movie star Marilyn Monroe exemplified the perfect woman of the 1950s and early 1960s. Monroe's weight changed over time, but she generally wore between a size ten and a size fourteen. Curves were definitely back in fashion.

Then in the 1960s, Monroe was replaced as an ideal by Twiggy, a British model. Twiggy was famous for having a stick-like figure. Once again, thin was in—and it has not really gone out of fashion since then.

With the rise of magazines like *Playgirl* in the 1970s, male models began appearing more often with less clothing. Men's bodies were now subjected to public scrutiny similar to that given to women's bodies. Up until this point, attention had been paid to men's strength and muscular builds as a way to project manliness or their ability to provide for a family. Instead, in the latter half of the twentieth century, average men began to concern themselves more with how their own bodies looked compared to the images they saw.

Since the 1980s, media images of both women and men portray sculpted, toned, and fit bodies, not just skinny ones. Unfortunately, recent published images of chiseled bodies have questionable forms of help: image manipulation, over-dieting, and drug use, such as anabolic steroids. In addition to the evolution of body ideals, technology and photography have also evolved. Very few model photos in the media are untouched.

Double Standard

The Kellogg Company conducted a survey of five thousand students in 1988–89. The survey showed that "almost one third of school-age children [grades three through twelve] believed they

Though teenage boys tend to be more accepting of their own bodies than girls are, they still value strength and athleticism.

were overweight."[5] This percentage is higher than the percentage of kids who are actually overweight.

However, male teenagers in grades nine through twelve who responded to the Kellogg survey were much more likely (86 percent) than females (66 percent) to describe themselves as the "right weight" or "underweight." Almost half (44 percent) of the girls were trying to lose weight at the time of the study, but only 15 percent of the boys were dieting at the time. Even one fourth of the girls who thought they weighed the right amount had tried to lose weight. Many of them used unhealthy ways to do it, by skipping meals, taking diet pills, or trying to throw up.[6]

A study published in the July–August 2003 issue of the *American Journal of Health Behavior* found that high-school girls see themselves as an average of eleven pounds over their ideal weight. However, the study, conducted by Dr. Michael Peterson, found that high-school boys' ideal body weight and their current body weight were about the same. Not only that, but many boys wanted to be heavier.[7] Many boys equated being heavy with being muscular or powerful. This perception is one thing that has led to the high use of steroids by teenage boys, especially athletes.

Puberty

As kids enter puberty, their bodies begin to occupy much of their thoughts. They need to get to know this strange body that has their head attached to it. The body that they did not need to think about much seems to suddenly change overnight.

Luckily, this does not really happen. Most people have a while to get used to their new bodies. One teenage girl wrote in her diary on her thirteenth birthday that she was depressed because she had not started developing yet and that the kids made fun of her. A year later, she wrote in her new diary that

What Exactly Happens at Puberty?

The chart below demonstrates the typical ages for body changes at puberty (based on a 1990s study of North Americans).[8]

Change	Average Age	Age Range
Girls:		
Breast "buds" form	10	8–13
Height spurt starts	10	8–13
Peak of strength spurt	10.5	8–14
First menstruation occurs	11.7	10–13.5
Adult stature reached	13	10–16
Breast growth completed	14	10–16
Pubic hair growth ends	14.5	14–15
Boys:		
Testes begin to enlarge	11.5	9.5–13.5
Pubic hair appears	12	10–15
Penis begins to enlarge	12	10.5–16
Height spurt begins	12.5	10.5–16
First ejaculation occurs	13	12–16
Peak of height spurt	14	12.5–15.5
Facial hair begins to grow	14	12.5–15.5
Voice begins to deepen	14	12.5–15.5
Penis growth completed	14.5	12.5–16
Peak of strength spurt	15.3	13–17
Adult stature reached	15.5	13.5–17.5
Pubic hair growth ends	15.5	14–17

she was depressed because she wore a 34DD bra and that the kids made fun of her.

"I used to lie in my bed at night and listen to her skin stretch," jokes her older brother, himself a teenager at the time.[9]

Meanwhile, boys are going through their own changes. According to Drs. Dan Kindlon and Michael Thompson, many adolescent boys wake up each morning with an uninvited erection:

> The feeling is often "Look what *it* can do" . . . a reflection of the way a boy views his instrument of sexuality as just that: an object. . . . The first experience of objectification of sexuality in a boy's life comes from his experience of his own body, having this penis that makes its own demands.[10]

You *Can* Be Too Thin

There is a saying, "You can never be too rich or too thin." Usually this saying is associated with females. As many as one out of every ten kids with an eating disorder is a boy. However, many people overlook eating disorders in boys.

Researcher Michael Peterson noted that teenagers' fascination with being thin contributes to many physical and mental health problems. Such beliefs can lead to eating disorders like anorexia nervosa and bulimia nervosa. Anorexia is an eating disorder in which people try to starve themselves because they believe they are too fat. Bulimia is a disorder where people overeat and then go to extreme measures to get rid of the food, often by making themselves vomit after overeating or taking excessive amounts of laxatives. This activity is known as bingeing and purging. It can cause severe damage to the throat, teeth, and digestive tract.

"We have seen a rise in eating disorders in both sexes, as well as a decrease in age at first appearance," says Dr. Toni Cottongim, a family physician in Cincinnati. "I talked to a twelve-year-old girl today who was worried about her 'belly pooch.' The kid was of normal height and weight for her age!" Dr. Cottongim and the other doctors in her practice are also seeing more young males who are worried excessively about their weight.[11]

"Body image issues are at an all-time high," says Dr. Michael Wilmington, a staff pediatrician for Kaiser Permanente. Dr. Wilmington feels that with our current emphasis on privacy, kids are not able to see average or typical bodies around them. Houses are bigger, with private bathrooms. Many schools no longer have open showers in locker rooms.

"So all the old ways kids learned what everyone looked like [have] disappeared," Dr. Wilmington says. He worries about where teenagers are getting their ideas of what "average" should look like. He says that he hears from his young female patients

> Among teenagers surveyed, boys were much less likely than girls to see themselves as overweight. Over 40 percent of the girls were dieting, compared with only 15 percent of the boys.

that they are having sex just to see what a real penis looks like. Similarly, Wilmington's young male patients tell him that they buy girlie magazines to see what women's bodies look like.

"Unfortunately the source is not [a] very reliable picture of girls at school," says Dr. Wilmington. "This sets the girls up with impossibly high standards to copy."[12] Many images of women on the Internet and in magazines start with a model who weighs, on average, 23 to 27 percent less than her non-model counterpart. Then the images are airbrushed, taking out pimples, dimples, and wrinkles. No wonder that boys are often disappointed with the girls they see in school. Those artificial expectations and disappointment then further feed the girls' unrealistic self-images.

Body Image

Body image is not just about weight and size—it is also about such factors as hair and facial features. However, having a positive body image and having an attractive appearance are not the same thing. People vary a great deal not just in how they think about their bodies but in how attractive their bodies actually are. Body image relates to how you *think* you look, which is a function of a number of things, including feedback from family, friends, and the media.

McLean Hospital in Massachusetts has developed a program to help teenage girls develop better images of themselves. "Full of Ourselves: Advancing Girl Power, Health and Leadership" stresses "girls' personal power and overall mental and physical well being."[13] Girls—and boys—can become so worried about what their bodies look like that they do not want to see anyone. They might have been teased by other kids or teens. Perhaps they were never actually teased; they might just be afraid that someone will be thinking bad things about what they look like. If teens are so worried about their body image that they will not go out, then they need help.

Virtual Relationships

One way that some people avoid facing their fears is by making cyber friendships. That way, they can pretend to look however they want to look. No one can tell. However, personal contact is important. People who interact only through a computer often lose their social skills. IMing, text messaging, and e-mails emphasize brevity of communication, not depth of understanding. Kids who rely on the Internet for virtual friendships often withdraw from real relationships with family and friends.

There might seem to be less risk of rejection when dealing with people through a computer intermediary. They cannot see your flaws unless you reveal them. However, true friendships are those that face the flaws in each other and embrace them. How

Carrying on a relationship in cyberspace can be easier than doing it in person. Some teens seem to communicate best through IM and e-mail.

secure can a relationship be if it is only allowed to see the good things and is never tested?

Popularity

Morgan (15), by IM: *"[Popularity] has the biggest impact on a girls life . . . how guys respond 2 u its awful . . . [that's] why girls are so worried abt thselves because guys are [jerks]."*[14]

Sometimes teenagers misunderstand what other people feel about them. Psychologist Dr. Linda Sonna says that too many teenagers "define their self-worth almost exclusively in terms of what their peers think of them—or in terms of what they *think* their peers think of them."[15]

Even the popular kids—or *especially* the popular kids—obsess about popularity. The king (or queen) of the hill worries about who is climbing up to knock him or her off the heap. Witness this instant message from Morgan, a very popular eighth grader:

Well [popularity] can be mean sometimes . . . cuz ppl are always telling u what 2 do and u always get named and its not all its cracked up 2 b I mean really u get the hott guy im mean ive been there done that but there is always something better abt the different guy. An I dont think that teens should focus on being popular they should focus on doing right because when u strive for something like being popular there are a lot of lies told and u can hurt urself and other ppl![16]

Popularity and friendship are not the same. As discussed earlier, popularity means being liked by a group of people. It can be very superficial, however. On the other hand, a person may be quite content with just a couple of very good friends. There is no right or wrong way to be. It depends on the individual person's needs.

Gender Identity and Sexual Orientation

Years ago, people thought that animals could easily be divided into two genders: male and female. However, recent research suggests that gender is not just an either/or choice. This research indicates that gender could be more of a continuum, with "male" at one end and "female" at the other. How male or female we appear is a combination of many things, including genetics, hormones, and environmental factors.

As children, our thoughts about gender are usually related to which restroom to use and who was allowed to come to our birthday parties because they did not have cooties that week.

As kids mature and approach puberty, however, they begin to think more about gender—their own and others'.

Gender Identity

Gender identity refers to how a person sees himself or herself, as masculine or feminine. This perception might not match what the rest of the world sees. For the majority of people, their gender identity is the same as their sex—that is, whether they are physically male or female.

In the 1960s, a psychologist by the name of John Money argued that people's gender identity was determined by how they were treated. He believed that gender identity was a "social construct," that *nurture* was more important than *nature*. However, recent research and experience have called his ideas into question.

Our chromosomes factor into gender identity. This is called our genotype—what our genetic makeup is. Our mother's eggs all carried one X chromosome. Our father's sperm carried either an X or a Y chromosome. When the sperm fertilizes the egg, the resulting embryo then carries either an XX or XY combination. Thus, the father determines a child's gender.

Another gender identity factor that affects maleness or femaleness is hormones. Testosterone is the dominant hormone in men and occurs in low amounts in women. Estrogen is the dominant hormone in women, but it, too, is found in both males and females.

Hormones affect us while in the womb. During the first three months of development, one gene on the Y chromosome of a male embryo causes a surge in male hormones (androgens). Likewise, a female embryo experiences a bath of female hormones (endrogens). These "hormone washes" help determine the development and appearance of male or female bodies.[1] After birth, hormones continue to affect us, especially at certain times of our lives: puberty, pregnancy, and menopause, for example.

The presence or absence of male or female genitalia also plays into gender identity. These are physical signs of gender to others: penis, testes, clitoris, and vulva. Although we cannot see them, girls also have a uterus, ovaries, and fallopian tubes. These physical signs help children develop their own sense of gender identity.

Transgender refers to people whose gender identity differs from the body they were born with. Sometimes people use it as a catchall term that includes transnaturals and transsexuals as well as gays and lesbians, but this is incorrect.

Transsexuals are people who identify with what appears to be their gender opposite. Sometimes children just feel that they were born the wrong gender. For example, a girl might have been born with a vagina and all the right female parts, but in her head she feels like a boy. She might feel attracted to girls (depending on the age). This is not the same as being a lesbian. Lesbian are truly female and feel, think, and act like females. However, they are attracted to people of the same gender.

Transsexuals often consider "gender reassignment" through hormone therapy and genital surgery. Gender reassignment is a long, involved, and expensive process to change someone's body from the gender it is to the gender with which he or she identifies. Because the process is so complicated and expensive, it is not an option for many people.

Transnaturals are people who identify with the opposite gender but have decided not to have genital surgery.

Intersexuals are those whose gender is not clear when they are born. They have genitals of both genders. This occurs in about one baby for every one hundred born. Such babies are often assigned a gender at birth. Assignment can lead to problems if the doctor doing the assigning picks the wrong gender. Before the word *intersexual* was used, the word *hermaphrodite* described people who had the genitals of both genders. Intersexual is the preferred term now.

The Intersex Society of North America (ISNA) was founded by Cheryl Chase, who was called a hermaphrodite when she was born. John Colapinto described meeting Chase in his book *As Nature Made Him: The Boy Who Was Raised as a Girl.* Colapinto writes: "To meet Chase and members of ISNA . . . is to enter a world where it is impossible to think of sex with the binary boy-girl, man-woman distinction we're accustomed to."[2]

Dr. D. F. Swaab, from the Netherlands, conducted research in the area of gender identity by examining the brain. He found that a certain area of the brains of male-to-female transsexuals (men who feel they should rightly be women) was the size it

From a very young age, children have strong ideas about what it means to be male or female.

normally was in women. In female-to-male transsexuals, the same area was the size it normally was in men. Swaab interpreted this to mean that females who felt they should have been male had male brains, and males who felt they should have been female had female brains. Swaab's findings were some of the first scientific research that supported the theory that some people's brains do not reflect their apparent gender.[3]

Sexual Orientation

Sexual orientation refers to the gender to which a person is attracted.[4] Other terms for this concept include *sexual identity* and *sexual preference*. To many people, the latter phrase implies that sexual attraction is a matter of conscious choice. For that reason, most people in the lesbian, gay, bisexual, transgendered/transsexual, or queer/questioning (LGBTQ) community prefer the term *sexual orientation.*

Men who appear to be male (and think of themselves as male) who are attracted to women who appear female (and think of themselves as female) are considered to be heterosexual. *Hetero* is from a Latin word meaning "different" or "opposite." That is, one sex attracted to the other sex. Another word for heterosexual that is often used is *straight.*

Homosexual, a term that has fallen out of favor, comes from the Latin word *homo,* which means "same." Therefore the term *homosexual* was used to describe men who look male and think of themselves as male who are attracted to other men. The same term is applied to women who look female and think of themselves as female who are attracted to other women. Acceptable words used now are *gay, lesbian,* and *bisexual.* Gay can refer to men or women. Lesbian refers to women only. Bisexual refers to people who are attracted to both genders.

How we see ourselves and to whom we are attracted is a complicated matter. One of the debates affecting both gender identity and sexual orientation is that of "nature versus nurture."

This is also referred to as "biology versus choice." Nature, or biology, refers to the idea that some people feel that your sexual orientation is based on how you were born and is beyond your control. Others believe that your sexual orientation comes from the way you were raised or choices that you have made on your own. Their nurture, or choice, point of view states that sexual orientation is based on environment.

Acceptance is important for most teens. Gay teens can experience this acceptance in gay peer groups and in support groups made up of both gay and straight students. In the safety of those groups, the teens' sexuality does not have to be hidden.[5]

Ann Heron is the editor of the book *Two Teenagers in Twenty: Writings by Gay and Lesbian Youth*. (The title refers to the proportion of people in the population that some researchers say are gay.) Heron noted that groups for gay teens are not growing as fast as they are needed:

> There's been some growth in support groups available to gay teenagers, but it hasn't kept pace with the number of teens who are confronting issues of sexual orientation. The sense of isolation and despair in the stories I received in 1993 was in fact even stronger than a decade ago.[6]

This sentiment is echoed by now twenty-eight-year-old Troix-Reginald Bennett. When he was eighteen, he wrote in *Two Teenagers in Twenty*,

> The fight remains, though. After coming out and establishing a life where we feel comfortable with ourselves, we tend to forget about the isolation and loneliness. We forget about those who aren't as lucky. I made it through, but what about all the other kids who fall between the cracks? Gay kids need access to housing, jobs, education, health care, counseling, and legal support. We need the help of the adult gay community to provide these services. We can't do this on our own. I was lucky to have someone to turn to. Most kids aren't so lucky.[7]

Gay-straight alliances can support gay teens, offering them a place of safety and respect. In 2000, these young people rallied in the sixth annual Gay/Straight Youth Pride March held in Boston.

Homosexuality

Much research has indicated that sexual attraction is more of a continuum than an absolute choice between two options. Sexual orientation and sexual behavior (which are not the same thing) vary over a range. Dr. Alfred Kinsey conducted research in the sexual practices of thousands of adolescents and adults. According to Kinsey's findings, very few people are permanently and exclusively homosexual or heterosexual.[8] Many people, especially teenagers, feel sexual attraction to someone of the same gender. That does not necessarily mean that they are or are not homosexual. In *What's Happening to My Body*, author Lynda Madaras says:

> Almost everyone has homosexual thoughts, feelings, fantasies, or experiences at some time or another in their lives. That's why we usually consider people to be homosexual only if, as adults, their strongest romantic and sexual attractions are toward someone of the same sex.[9]

So, are gay or lesbian people born to love people of the same gender? Or did they consciously or subconsciously *choose* to love someone of the same gender? Many people focus only on the sex act itself when discussing homosexuality. As with heterosexual relationships, there is more than just sex involved. Many gay and lesbian couples have been together for decades. The relationship is built around such things as trust, love, security, and companionship—not just sex.

Is sexual identity by chance or by choice? Many people say that homosexuality is not natural. They say that nature needs species to continue. Any species, to endure, needs to procreate—to have babies. Without procreation, the species would naturally die out. Therefore, these people argue, it is not nature's intention for people to couple with others of the same gender. Gay and lesbian couples can have children, but not without some outside intervention. (Of course, many heterosexual couples need outside intervention to have babies, too.)

There are animals that are naturally attracted to animals of the same gender, both in nature and in captivity. Zoos all over the world have had many faithful same-sex pairs. In both Germany and New York, zoos had to concede that their gay male penguins were not interested in the other gender, no matter how many female penguins they introduced them to. One New York pair, Roy and Silo, even hatched an egg—an extra from another pair of penguins—and raised a chick together.[10]

The American Psychiatric Association (APA) publishes the *Diagnostic and Statistical Manual of Mental Disorders*, which describes thousands of psychological problems. In 1973, the APA removed homosexuality from the list of disorders or diseases in the manual, saying that homosexuality was not a problem that needed to be fixed. The APA polled its members; the vote was 5,834 for removal and 3,810 against.[11] (Today, over thirty years later, it seems likely that the vote would be even more lopsided.) According to the APA, "The action was taken following a review of the scientific literature and consultation with experts in the field. The experts found that homosexuality does not meet the criteria to be considered a mental illness."[12] Although all major mental health organizations are in accord with the APA's stance, some people still do not agree.

In 1992, the APA further strengthened its stance on homosexuality when it called for measures to end prosecution and persecution of gay people: "The APA calls on these organizations and individuals to do all that is possible to decrease the stigma related to homosexuality wherever and whenever it may occur."[13]

> Gender identity refers to whether people view themselves as male or female. It is different from sexual orientation, which refers to whether people are attracted to the same or the opposite sex.

There is also the sad reality that gay people often face many difficulties, from family rejection to discrimination in society. People have been attacked and even murdered simply because they are gay. "Seth," an Ohio college student, says, "I would not have *chosen* to love a lifestyle where I would be shunned, made fun of, abused and rejected. I doubt anyone would *choose* that."[14]

Coming Out

The act of telling others that you are gay is called coming out. It refers to "coming out of the closet," meaning choosing not to live a life in secret that must be hidden—in a closet.

Kids who feel that they are gay face tough choices. Do I tell anybody? Whom do I tell? How do I tell them—and when? Most often the first step is to come out to yourself. Nineteen-year-old David writes in *Two Teenagers in Twenty*,

> Perhaps the most difficult part of this process is realizing and admitting, "I am gay." In my case, there was a gradual awareness that I was different from everyone else. . . . After a long period of self-hatred, I came to realize that every human being has an inherent beauty. Therefore, some unique beauty existed within me, and I had a contribution to make to the world.[15]

After you have come out to yourself, you need to consider who else you want to tell—and when. Coming out is a lifelong process, as each time a gay person makes a new friendship, the decision has to be made over again: Do I tell?

The experience of coming out to one's parents can be difficult on both sides. In *Prayers for Bobby*, author Leroy Aarons describes how Bobby felt the night he came out to his mother: "Worst of all, the revelation had blown apart the intimate familial contract; for all his family's protestations of love, the bubble had ruptured and Bobby was on the outside looking in."[16]

On the other hand, the coming-out process can begin negatively and end in affirmation. When Fran Kirschner and her husband, Allen, received a letter from their daughter Kerry telling them that she was a lesbian, Fran said:

> I cried and cried and cried. . . . The discrimination, the bigotry, the hate they will face. I think that's the majority of the tears. [But] there's nothing wrong with my daughter. She's a beautiful young woman. . . . [I don't want to] give the impression that I am embarrassed by . . . my daughter. Nothing could be further from the truth.[17]

One thing for teens to consider is what reaction they *need* to get. They'll also need to anticipate the reaction they *expect* to get. Teens about to come out to someone should try to figure out how the person will react. One strategy is to bring up

Some animals, such as penguins, form pair bonds with members of the same gender. Some people point to this as support for a biological basis for homosexuality.

famous gay people or characters and see how the person reacts to that. Also, teens should keep in mind the length of time it took them to come to grips themselves with their sexual orientation and give others time to digest the information, too.[18]

Teens who are considering coming out to someone should ask themselves these questions first:

• Am I certain enough about my sexual orientation that I want to label myself at this point in my life? Some young people find that they "experiment" with people of the same gender but find it is not the right lifestyle for them.

- Have *I* accepted my sexuality? Am I comfortable enough with it to discuss it with another person? Some teens find that the people they tell try to "talk them out of it," which can make them get defensive or send off mixed signals. This then can encourage him or her to continue trying to talk the gay teen into being something (or someone) else.

- Do I have the support of someone else, or is this the first person in whom I'm confiding? Of course, the first time might be the most difficult. It depends on whether you pick someone who means a lot to you or not. Coming out first to someone whose opinion you do not value might seem less threatening but might not be the best choice.

- Is this solely my decision? Do I have another person who is pushing me to come out before I'm ready?

LGBTQ Kids and Schools

The Hetrick-Martin Institute was formed originally as the Institute for Protection of Lesbian and Gay Youth. Psychiatrist Emery S. Hetrick and professor A. Damien Martin formed the institute after a fifteen-year-old boy was assaulted and beaten, then thrown out of the group home he was living in. He was blamed for causing the incident because he was gay.[19]

The good news is that many schools are forming gay-straight alliances (GSAs). The Gay-Straight Alliance network was founded in 1998 to help connect school-based GSAs to one another and to resources in their communities. The group was successful, for example, in achieving an agreement for one school district to enact mandatory teacher and student training.[20]

Asexuality—Neither, Please

Before the 1960s, many gays and lesbians chose to live a celibate life rather than to come out of the closet. (People who are celibate do not have sex.) However, we cannot assume that every person who chooses to live his or her life in apparent celibacy is homosexual. There are many reasons for choosing celibacy. Some people choose to be celibate because they are not married. Others choose celibacy as members of a religious order. And some people feel no sexual drive. People who do not experience sexual attraction—or do not feel compelled to act upon any sexual attraction they might feel—are called asexual.

As with homosexuality, asexuality has sometimes been seen as a bad or undesirable condition that must be "fixed." Hypoactive sexual desire disorder is one of the disorders currently listed in the fourth edition of the *Diagnostic and Statistical Manual of Mental Disorders.* ("Hypoactive" means less active than normal.) Psychiatrists caution that a lack of sexual desire due to other causes, such as illness, must first be ruled out. Also, it is defined as a disorder if the lack of sexual desire is causing other problems, such as problems within a relationship.[21]

People who describe themselves as being asexual often say that their first thoughts were that something was wrong with them. David Jay is an asexual man who in 2001 formed Asexual Visibility and Education Network (AVEN). Through AVEN, more than twelve hundred people have begun networking to share their experiences. One seventeen-year-old described looking up the word *asexual* in the dictionary when she was fifteen.

"If there were a word for what I'm starting to think I am, it wouldn't—unlike . . . homosexual, heterosexual, bisexual, transsexual—it wouldn't have the word 'sex' in it," she wrote in her journal. "I'm something different."[22]

Defining our sexuality often occurs as we are becoming attracted to someone else. That attraction we feel often helps us define who we are.

5 Special Relationships—When Boy Friends Become Boyfriends

Romantic relationships can start in many ways. Often the best relationships start out as friendships. Ericka Lutz, in her book *The Complete Idiot's Guide to Friendship for Teens*, includes a whole chapter entitled "How to Take the Road from Friendship to Romance and Back Again."[1]

Lutz's book exemplifies something that has not changed over the years. Mainstream magazines aimed at teenagers still tend to emphasize an old-fashioned approach to romance. Melissa Glass's article in the June/July 2004 issue of *Teen People* is typical: "How to go from Crush to Couple: 7 Steps to Boyfriend

Bliss." The article comes complete with sidebars on "Dating Don'ts" and "The Perfect Kiss."[2]

Dating at Different Ages

When two adolescents are trying to establish a romantic relationship, raging hormones can make it difficult, not to mention immaturity, problems communicating, and different needs between the two. Also, boys and girls develop at different rates. A girl matures sooner, which might make older boys more appealing to her. Frequently a boy her age is not interested in dating yet. Chances are also good that she has already reached her peak height by the age of thirteen. As the table in Chapter 4 shows, boys do not reach their adult height until around fifteen and a half, on average, so they probably look up to girls their own age—at least literally.

As girls pass from their "tween" years to their teen years, many changes are taking place. Their relationships with boys can begin to be more important than their relationships with girls. If one girl is more successful at or concerned with dating boys, then that can strain her relationship with another girl. Many girls will often pretend to be something they are not in order to catch the attention of a boy they are interested in. And her friends will notice. The most common pretense is trying to act less smart, as girls become afraid of "scaring away" a boy with their brains. Even girls who are attracted to other girls will find themselves going through some of the same phases, as they strive to put someone else's desires first before their own. No matter whether a girl is straight or gay, she will probably form many relationships with boys. Some of those relationships can be built on pure friendship and nothing more.[3]

Sometimes an older person seems more attractive (perhaps more stable, too). There can be danger in this attraction, however, if the age difference crosses the "age of consent" boundary. (The age of consent is the age at which a person is considered

The Return of Courtship?

Members of some religious groups in the United States, including some conservative Christians, advocate the practice of courtship rather than dating. That is, they say it is best for couples to get to know each other under the supervision of their parents with marriage as the goal. Such couples do not spend time alone in private, and often they do not do so much as kiss until after the wedding.

The reasoning behind this is that dating, with its casual romance and numerous partners, leads to emotional pain and the possibility of premarital sex. Supporters of a return to courtship cite the high rate of divorce in this country as evidence that conventional forms of dating are a failure. Something different is needed, they say, to establish close, permanent, godly relationships.

According to Brad A. Voyles, dean of student life at Belhaven College in Mississippi:

> There has been a big movement in the last several years of people going back to the old courtship model. You talk to the parents to get permission to date the daughter, you don't go on dates by yourself but with groups of people, and dating is for the purpose of getting to know the other person with designs on getting married.[4]

One couple who took this approach is Casey Moss and Kara Price, who became "betrothed" in a church ceremony when she was fourteen and he was twenty. As Moss described their relationship: "I can begin to emotionally connect because it's safe. (She's) not going to leave in six months and break my heart. . . . There's a real sense of security because no matter how rough it gets, we're stuck together. It's nice. It's very nice."[5]

mature enough to be able to consent on his or her own to sexual relations. For most states, the age of consent is sixteen.)

What the age of consent laws mean is that in most states, if a girl is fifteen and her boyfriend is seventeen, if they have sex he can be arrested for statutory rape—even if she wanted to and agreed to have sex with him. She is considered by the law to be too young to be able to agree. Sometimes, this is a situation in which there does not seem to be a victim, and no one seemed to be harmed, but the person who is above the age of consent can be arrested, charged, and successfully convicted. Sometimes it is the boy who is under the age of consent and the girl who is older, but this is less common.

Marriage laws also tend to follow the age of consent, but they vary by state and whether the parents have given permission. Without parental consent, most states will not allow teenagers younger than eighteen to marry.[6] Some states will allow teenagers to get married without parental permission if the girl is pregnant and has a doctor's order proving it. The youngest age to get married under any circumstances in this country is twelve.[7]

Relationships Through the Ages

A study of relationships across the ages and across cultures reveals a consistent double standard. For the most part, women have been expected to be sexually pure—virginal before marriage and faithful afterward. In contrast, men have been expected to express their masculinity through sexual activity.

In ancient times, a girl was often betrothed to a much older man as a way to seal a relationship between her family and his. This practice continues in some cultures today. Children usually came right away and were often needed as contributors to the family farm or business.

The economy of marriage is seen in the terms *trousseau* and *dowry*. These refer to the possessions that the bride brings to a

Dating Customs Around the World

Not all teenagers socialize by going to the movies or the mall. Dating customs differ greatly from country to country. Here's a sample:

Iran: By law, teens are not allowed to date in Iran. When they are of marriageable age, their families introduce them to potential spouses.

Afghanistan: Boys and girls go to different schools, so there is little mixing between the sexes. Marriages are arranged by the young people's families.

Japan: Most teenagers do not date until they graduate from high school. Men invite women on dates and pay for everything.

Finland: Teens tend to go out in large groups.

Spain: Spanish teenagers usually go out one-on-one. Either the boy or the girl can ask the other out, and they split the cost of the date. In both Spain and Latin America, girls do not date before they celebrate their *quinceañera*, or fifteenth birthday.

Russia: Teenagers often go in large groups to dance clubs and coffeehouses.

Australia: Young Australian teens usually go out in groups. Among older teens, both sexes initiate the date and either can pay.[8]

Sometimes the best romantic relationships start out as friendships.

marriage. Sometimes the bride does not bring the possessions to the marriage itself but to the groom's parents. Even today in many Asian and African cultures, the engagement is negotiated as a business deal between the two families.

In ancient times, especially during times of war, men would travel to other villages to kidnap women to become their wives. Some warriors would rape the women and leave them behind. In this way, they hoped to terrify and subdue their enemies as well as spread their influence. The father might never be known to the child or its mother. Because of this practice, to this day

Marriage customs in early America were quite different from those today, as this painting of a colonial-era proposal shows.

teenagers were either married or quickly became married before the birth of the baby, who was frequently announced to be "premature" by the family, if not the doctor. Group activities seemed to allay parents' fears that their children would be among the statistics of teenage parents.[10]

Heath says:

> Perhaps group social events seemed less threatening to adults who might have feared that young people were "not ready" to form unions that implied a permanent commitment. I also see an age variation—the teen canteens definitely appeared to attract a contingent of younger teenagers (usually under age 16 or 17, but that line was not firm). On the other hand, movie theaters and "lovers' lanes" were obviously locales that older teens or young college students might frequent.[11]

Even after World War II, however, Heath has noted signs of people just "going out" as opposed to "going steady." The former was just dating for fun. The latter meant dating one person to the exclusion of all others.

"As for the 1960s and after—again, there are some trends that we might consider," says Heath:

> First, the social changes associated with the so-called "sexual revolution" (and accompanying government approval of the first oral contraceptives) might have loosened the bonds of matrimony, or at least the moral and social standards associated with finding someone to commit to.[12]

Forming Relationships

If you think that you might be interested in someone, it can be hard to figure out what to do next. There are many different ways for relationships to begin. For instance, in *What's Happening to My Body*, author Lynda Madaras describes how many relationships come from friendships that develop into crushes. She makes a distinction between "unrealistic" crushes, such as those on movie stars or singers, and "realistic" crushes. Realistic crushes are on

Amish Teens: Black Caps and Buggy Rides

The Amish are closely knit religious and cultural groups who have lived in the United States since the eighteenth century, mainly in rural Pennsylvania, New York, and the Midwest. They live simply, without many modern inventions, such as cars, electricity, and—in some cases—buttons. The Amish are known for their beautiful farms, quilts, and horse-drawn buggies. Children attend Amish schools through the eighth grade; at that point they begin their working lives.

Though practices differ from one community to another, those of the Old Order Amish in Arthur, Illinois, are a good example of Amish customs. In this group, young people begin dating at about the age of sixteen. Because they have not yet become baptized members of the church, the teens do not have to follow all the rules their elders do. They can listen to music, wear modern clothing, and visit cities. This time of life is called *rumspringa*, which translates as "running around."

On Saturday nights—date night—teens go on buggy rides, play games in groups, or spend time as couples at home. According to Lindsey MacAllister, a historian, "Boys wait until a girl's parents retire for the evening before visiting. . . . Dating allows a boy and girl to spend an extended amount of time together."[13]

Amish girls who are ready to date make this known by wearing a black cap and a white apron with a cape. After a boy and girl have dated for a while, they often become a steady couple. MacAllister says, "Steady, long-term couples usually marry."[14] Most Amish youth join the church in their late teens, are baptized, and get married, thus becoming adult members of the community.

people with whom the person actually comes in contact and who might be a potential date.[15]

People can develop crushes on people of the same gender. One type of crush is based on wanting to identify with the object of your affection rather than on sexual attraction alone. This does not necessarily mean that either of you is or is not gay.[16]

The majority of crushes will most likely fade away and never go any further. Sometimes crushes develop into genuine sexual or romantic relationships. According to Dr. Michael Riera, first love is "an unparalleled phenomenon. Nothing can match it in terms of excitement, energy, and positive feelings."[17]

How Can I Tell Someone I'm Interested?

Author Rosalind Wiseman found when she studied teens that both boys and girls felt the best way to let someone know that you like him or her is to tell the person directly.[18] Do most teens do that? Of course not! Teens of both genders like to be involved in the drama of romance but might not yet have the nerve to approach someone directly. If someone approaches you and says he or she wants to tell you something on behalf of someone else, here are some thoughts to consider:

- Do you know for sure whether the messenger is speaking for someone else or for himself or herself?

- Is the messenger truthful?

- Does the messenger have a hidden agenda? That is, could he or she be telling you lies for some other reason?

- If the approach comes over the telephone, can you be sure that no one else is listening?

If you are tempted to ask someone else to deliver a romantic message for you—don't. Doing it yourself feels scarier, but there is actually less risk involved. At the very least, fewer people are

"Guess what I heard . . . ?" While it's tempting to have a third party deliver a message to someone you're interested in, it's often a better idea to do it yourself.

involved in your business. That means the communication might be clearer. It also means that fewer people can laugh at you if things go badly. In addition, you also stand to gain more than if you had someone else do your talking for you. The person you are approaching might really appreciate your willingness to take a chance.

If you like someone, you could break the ice by complimenting the person. People usually like to hear genuine compliments. You could ask the other person's opinion on something. Then make sure you listen to it. Get the other person to talk more than you talk. People like to be heard. You could also either help the other person with something or ask for help.

How Can I Tell Someone I'm *Not* Interested?

Think about the person who is asking you. How can you help this person save face? Here are a few suggestions about what to say:

- "I'm sorry, no" (and sound sorry).

- "Thank you for asking, but I'm already involved." (You do not have to say with what or with whom. Let them assume it is another person. You might be involved with reading.)

- "I don't think that's a good idea. Let's just stay friends."

- "Thank you so much for trusting me with your feelings. I don't want our relationship to change."

Breaking Up With Someone

Another time you might be tempted to use a messenger is when you want to break up with someone. Many people do use a messenger: instant messenger. Before you do this, however, ask yourself if it is right.

Breakups are painful and difficult most of the time, whether you are the "dumper" or the "dumpee." Sometimes it's easier to be dumped, because you are in a reactive mode. To dump someone else, you need to make the decision yourself, then summon up the courage to tell the other person. Here are some good ways to get started:

- "We need to talk."

- "I've got something on my mind that I would like to discuss."

- "Are you happy?"

Dancing and Dating

Another thing that is intimately intertwined with teenage dating is teenage dancing. In some African countries, young women signal their readiness to marry by participating in particular dances. In the United States, dancing has played a part in courtship since colonial times.

Dance cards, which document the tradition of dancing with many partners in one night, were popular from the late seventeenth to the middle twentieth century. Dance cards listed the songs to be played. Gentlemen signed up for dances on a lady's card until it was full. Her escort always got the first and last dance.

The ballroom-type dancing of the 1940s and 1950s reinforced the couple itself. On the other hand, some dancing styles of recent decades reinforce the group. Beginning in the 1960s, popular dances, such as the Frug, the Watusi, the Pony, and the Twist, often involved no touching. Sometimes it was difficult to look at a dance floor and be able to pick out who was dancing with whom.

"I noted a big change in young people's dating habits from the 1960s onward with shifting dance styles and social events," says Sarah Heath. "Slam dancing, and later 'raves,' or 'mosh pits' . . . seem much more conducive to that group identity rather than to couples dancing that was more common in the 1940s and 1950s."[19]

In disco dancing of the 1970s and 1980s, people went back to dancing with a partner. However, the partners might change as the night wore on. Two other styles of dancing emerged in the 1970s and 1980s, however, that went beyond the group dancing style of the 1960s. Disco included a type of line dancing, such as the Bus Stop. Not only did line dancing not require couples—it didn't even need members of both genders. Break dancing became popular with the rise of rap music in the 1980s. Also in the 1980s came another type of group dancing: country line dancing.

Dancing in the 1990s went back to more couples dancing, with a tendency to stay with one partner all night. Another influence on the movement back to couples was the Latino influence on dancing in the 1990s, especially with salsa dancing.

One thing has not changed, however, through the last five decades. Slow songs are for more intimate body movement, hanging on to one partner.

If you are the one being left behind, try not to respond with anger. This is easy to say and less easy to do. However, getting angry is not a productive use of your energy. Resist the urge to say something that will hurt the other person as much as you feel hurt. Many dating relationships are able to end as friendships, especially those that started out as friendships in the first place.

If your boyfriend or girlfriend has behaved violently in the past, be careful when you decide to break up. It might be wise to break up when you are in your territory, such as your home. An even better situation is if your parents or older siblings are nearby. Do not break up with someone who has a violent temper when you do not have a way out. Always make sure that you can get home.

> **Teens say the best way to let someone know you like him or her is to say so directly. However, not many find this easy to do.**

Going Out and Going With

In the 2000s, teens often go out in groups.[20] Their favorite hangouts are malls, movies, and video arcades. There are not necessarily any couples, just a group. Is this considered a date? Not really. But it's called going out. Going out in groups happens in many places besides the United States, including Sweden and Vietnam.[21]

At some point, teens start to pair up in couples and decide to go out just the two of them. Although some sixth graders are now going out on dates, they are often accompanied by a parent—at least for part of the time. After all, sixth graders cannot drive yet.

Then there is going *with* someone. In the 1950s up to the 2000s, this term usually referred to a couple that had dated each other exclusively. It also meant that they had not dated anyone else for some substantial amount of time, at least a few weeks.

This photograph, taken over a century ago, shows that styles of clothing change, but the desire to form connections does not.

In the 2000s, however, young teens go with another person just by announcing it to all their friends. They usually tell their friends who their boyfriend or girlfriend is. The breakup is also often done by announcement. Sometimes this can happen over the course of a school day—without setting foot off school grounds!

Going Steady

Going *steady* used to mean the same thing as going *with*. It meant that you were dating one person exclusively (and implied that you had already dated this person for a while before you made the decision to go steady). Going steady was often the step before engagement and then marriage. Often couples would exchange tokens of some sort. A boy would often give a girl his class ring; usually it was too big for the girl's finger, so she wore it on a necklace chain.

Now, however, going steady has taken on other meanings. In the past, going steady did not necessarily involve sexual relations, although it could. It definitely meant that couples were having sex only with each other, if at all. A recent study was conducted at the University of Cincinnati by researchers from the University of Texas Medical Branch at Galveston. The researchers found that 45 percent of teenage girls in the study had had simultaneous relationships with two boys. They also found that two thirds of them did not have intercourse with the secondary boy, even if they were doing so with the primary boyfriend.[22]

Coming Out and Going Out

Getting up your nerve to ask someone out is difficult. It is even trickier if you are gay. There is the usual possibility of rejection if the person does not want to go out with you. However, there is an added risk in that you might have approached someone who is not gay. Then you have risked being *outed* (revealed to be gay if you were not out before), losing a friendship, or being ridiculed.

TeenWire.com has advice for teens who are trying to negotiate two thorny fields: asserting their homosexuality and also attempting to ask someone out. One challenge that LGBTQ teens face is meeting other LGBTQ teens. One possibility is being introduced by a mutual friend. This has the added bonus of the personal testimony. The friend might also be able to confirm whether the other person is also LGBTQ. Teens could also meet LGBTQ teens through school. Urban schools usually have more potential partners than rural schools, because they tend to be bigger. They also have the bonus of some anonymity. If two teens are not out as a couple at their own school, they might find they can melt into the background at a bigger school. Most teens would not find it practical or possible to change schools based on sexual orientation, but sometimes bigger schools hold social functions where kids from other schools are invited.

Yet another way to meet other LGBTQ teens is online, of course, but this is risky.[23] The Counseling Center of the University of South Carolina in Aiken has created a "Coming Out Virtual Brochure." In it they address the multiple fears of LGBTQ teens about to come out and go out.

> For homosexual adolescents, the teen years through early twenties can be especially difficult. Along with the normal teen angst of hormones gone haywire and bodily changes, they have to deal with their insecurities concerning their sexual orientation, their fear of telling their families and friends, and the possibility of negative reactions to coming out, and society's prejudice and stigmatization towards homosexuality. This may increase a young homosexual person's feelings of distress and depression, lower their self-esteem, and could possibly lead them to engage in sexually risky behavior, such as multiple partners and unprotected sex.[24]

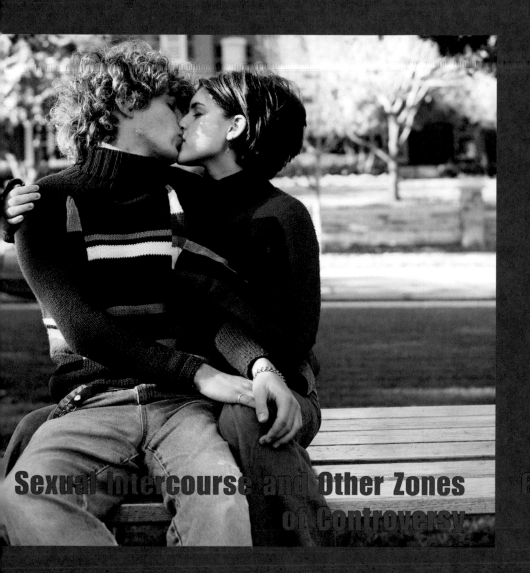

Morgan, by IM: *"Sex is a HUGE decision. . . . just go with what ur heart says its okay 2 be curious abt everything but u need 2 have sex when ur good and ready . . . for me chastity is a huge deal and I plan 2 b a virgin till im married . . . so im not gonna say DON'T HAVE SEX ima say have sex when ur ready 2 have sex . . . and don't be afraid 2 say no and don't be pressured in2 it."*[1]

Sex. Just three little letters, but a world of controversy revolves around them. Without sex, most species could not survive. Like some humans, some animals seek a lifelong mate with whom to raise children. But then humans went a step further

By the Numbers

- Fifty percent of sexually active teen males have their first sexual experience between ages eleven and thirteen.

- The birthrate in 1998 for children aged ten to fourteen was one birth per one thousand girls.

- Thirteen percent of all U.S. births are to teenagers. Approximately three quarters of teenage mothers are unmarried.

- Each year, 20 percent of sexually active teenage girls become pregnant.

- A sexually active teenage girl who does not use contraceptives has a 90 percent chance of becoming pregnant within one year.

- The mortality rate for infants born to teenage mothers is about 50 percent higher than that for those born to women over age twenty.

- The U.S. teenage birthrate is the highest in the developed world. This is due to fewer comprehensive sex education programs, less access to contraception and abortion, and fewer confidential services for teenagers.

- Every year about 25 percent of sexually active teenagers acquire a sexually transmitted disease.

- From a single act of unprotected sex with an infected partner, a teenage woman has a one percent risk of acquiring HIV, a 30 percent risk of getting genital herpes, and a 50 percent chance of contracting gonorrhea. Up to 29 percent of sexually active teenage girls and 10 percent of teenage boys tested for sexually transmitted diseases had chlamydia.[2]

with the self-awareness and conscience that only humans have. We invented marriage, which is a process involving paperwork, promises, and public professions of love and commitment. Is it necessary to be married to have sex? No. Is it a good idea? Many people think so.

Sexual intercourse involves emotions. When we become intimate, we can become vulnerable, so that we risk getting hurt by the other person. Sexual intercourse involves communication. We need to understand what our partner's assumptions, needs, and expectations are. Sexual intercourse involves the possibility of parenthood. Sexual intercourse involves the risk of disease. AIDS is the focus of a great deal of attention these days, but there are other diseases that are more easily contracted and kill more people each year than AIDS does. For example, there are six different strains of hepatitis. Hepatitis B is one hundred times easier to catch than AIDS. More people, worldwide, die from hepatitis B in one day than from AIDS in one year. There is no known cure for hepatitis B.[3]

Psychologist Linda Sonna says:

> There is also serious physical risk involved, since you could catch a disease or make a baby. You can lessen those risks by taking precautions, but there is a huge emotional risk, because when people have intercourse, they often develop a very strong attachment. If you later realize you do not like that person anymore or decide that the person is wrong for you, you may have a hard time ending the relationship because when you gave your body, you gave your heart, too.[4]

Intercourse

Having worked with many pregnant teenagers, I've yet to see one of them pregnant [because they got too much] information. It just doesn't happen. Kids are less likely to have intercourse in their teen years [than their peers] . . . if they are given good

information, have open communication with their parents, and
see their parents interacting in sexually healthy ways.

—Barbara Coloroso, U.S. parent educator and author[5]

In Coloroso's opinion, giving more teens information about intercourse does not lead to their being more likely to have sex. In addition, teens need to have information on a wide range of topics regarding sexuality—not just intercourse.

Why do people have sex? This question is not often asked during the heat of the moment. If it were, many people, especially teenagers, would realize that their reasoning is either faulty or nonexistent. Here are some statements made in an informal survey of adults who were asked their reasons for having sex as teenagers:

- I was in the mood.
- He was there and he expected it.
- To show her how much I love her.
- To keep him from going out with other people.
- I wanted to have a baby. I wanted someone to love just me.
- The movie was exciting.
- I was drunk.

Drinking alcohol is frequently blamed for sexual intercourse, both among teenagers (which is illegal) and among adults. Stedman Graham makes this point in his book *Move Without the Ball*:

Alcohol is the number one drug of choice for teens. By their senior year in high school, 80 percent of teens have tried alcohol, compared with 47 percent who have tried marijuana and 29 percent who have tried another illegal drug. But it doesn't fix anything. It doesn't make them cool, more attractive to the opposite sex, or more likely to be accepted by the "in" crowd. . . . For one thing, it leads to a huge increase in unprotected sex. Teens

Alcohol use is associated with lowered inhibitions. Sometimes this means unplanned sex.

who drink are seven times more likely to engage in sex and twice as likely to have sex with multiple partners than those who do not.[6]

Teenage pregnancy rates have fallen throughout the 1990s and 2000s. Two reasons are that a lower percentage of teenagers engage in sexual intercourse, and that a higher percentage of those who are engaging use birth control. According to an article in *The New York Times*, boys' choices are contributing to this change. "More than half of all male high school students reported in 2001 that they were virgins, up from 39 percent in 1990. Among the sexually active, condom use has soared to 65 percent, and nearly 73 percent among black male students."[7]

There still exists a double standard, however, as shown in a survey conducted by *Seventeen* magazine and the Kaiser Family Foundation. In it, 91 percent of teens surveyed said that girls can get a bad reputation for having sex, but only 42 percent of them said the same for boys.[8]

What Is Sex?

This seems like an easy enough question, but there are a number of different opinions. Some people define sex only as vaginal intercourse; others include oral sex and anal sex on the list. And for some, any genital touching qualifies.

According to Claude Allen, deputy secretary of Health and Human Services, "When we ask young people, 'Have you engaged in sexual activity?' we often hear, 'Well, what do you mean by that?'"[9]

One problem with this is that teens who define sex too narrowly may be taking risks as a result. For instance, half of all teens do not consider oral sex to be real sex. However, though oral sex obviously does not lead to pregnancy, it can spread STDs such as gonorrhea.

In addition to health issues are the emotional issues that are connected with sex. As college student Alice Kunce put it, "In high school, you could have oral sex and still call yourself a virgin. Now I'm like, 'Well, what makes one less intimate than the other?'"[10]

Outercourse

Besides less intercourse and more contraception, another change that might account for part of the decrease in teenage pregnancy is "outercourse." Outercourse refers to sexual activities that do not involve any form of penetration of the penis into the vagina. Some examples of outercourse are oral sex and mutual masturbation. Although there is little to no risk of pregnancy, however, there is still risk of disease. According to a report by The Alan Guttmacher Institute, an organization that conducts research on sexual and reproductive health issues:

> Saliva tends to inactivate the HIV virus, so while transmission through oral intercourse is not impossible, it is relatively rare. Other viral STDs that can be transmitted orally include human papillomavirus [HPV], herpes simplex virus and hepatitis B, while gonorrhea, syphilis, chlamydia and chancroid are among the bacterial infections that can be passed through oral sex.[11]

The Centers for Disease Control and Prevention conducted a survey in 2005 and found that more than half of teenagers had engaged in oral sex. In the *Seventeen*–Kaiser survey, only 58 percent of teenage males thought that oral sex was as serious as intercourse. However, 72 percent of the teenage females surveyed thought it was to be taken as seriously as intercourse.[12]

Dr. Elizabeth Casparian, who received her Ph.D. in human sexual behaviors, is concerned about teenagers who do not consider oral sex as serious as intercourse. "If they believe that [oral sex] isn't intimate, then they're not going to expect the emotional consequences that come along with participating in intimate human behavior." She says that if teens do not expect to experience emotional consequences but then do, that can result in confusion and loss of self-esteem.[13]

Masturbation

One way that people experience sexual pleasure is through masturbation. That means sexually stimulating oneself either with a hand or some other object. Some people like to look at images that arouse them while masturbating. Couples sometimes stimulate each other this way before, after, or instead of intercourse. Some people find that they cannot reach orgasm through regular intercourse. An orgasm is the intense, explosive sensation that occurs at the climax of sexual excitement; it is accompanied by ejaculation in the male. The muscles tighten and release all at once. Some people compare it to the feeling you get at the top of a roller coaster when you are tense with excitement and you know the fall is inevitable. The physical feeling has been described as being like a sneeze. One French phrase for orgasm translates to "little death" in English.

Is masturbation healthy? Is it bad? Some religious groups oppose masturbation, but modern scholarship has shown that the arguments against it are not in the Bible. Masturbation can be a way of getting acquainted with your own body and finding out what is pleasurable. This can help provide better sexual encounters with a partner because you know your own body better. Masturbation can also release tension. It can be fine. It can be fun. It should take place in private, either alone or with a partner, however.

Contraception

Contraception and some of the views about it have changed over the years. For example, in 1873 the U.S. Comstock Law said that all contraceptive devices and information about them, as well as information about abortion, were obscene. Less than one hundred years later, the Food and Drug Administration approved the first birth control pill in 1960. "The Pill," as it quickly became known, helped spark the sexual revolution of the 1960s. For the first time ever, women had a reliable way of controlling conception. This freedom affected both men and women.

The Pill and Other Hormonal Methods

Many women prefer to use methods that involve taking something orally. There are different formulas for birth control pills. The most common pill contains a combination of estrogen (a female hormone) and progestin (a synthetic form of the hormone progesterone, which is produced by the woman's ovaries). This dose of hormones prevents a woman from ovulating. She will have menstrual periods as usual, but no egg will be released.[14] One of the pleasant side effects of the combination pill is that it often makes a woman's periods lighter, more regular, and less painful. Some of the unpleasant side effects include possible weight gain, breast tenderness, and headaches. A second kind of

The birth control pill, introduced in the 1960s, was the first highly reliable form of contraception. It brought about a significant change in attitudes and behavior with regard to sex.

pill contains progestin alone. This causes the cervical mucus to thicken, which keeps sperm from reaching the egg.

The pill is effective if used as directed, but some women find they have trouble remembering to take it every day. Any contraceptive method is only as effective as the person is diligent in using it.

Several other types of contraceptives also work on the basis of hormones introduced in the woman's body: a shot given once every three months; a ring that a woman inserts vaginally and leaves in place for a month; and a weekly patch that adheres to the skin. Both the ring and the patch secrete hormones that prevent pregnancy.

Teenage pregnancy rates have fallen for the last decade because a lower percentage of teens are having sexual intercourse—and those who do are more likely to use birth control.

The Condom

One contraceptive device that has been around for a long time is the condom. It fits over the penis and prevents sperm from entering the vagina. Condoms became popular after the process for vulcanizing rubber was perfected in the 1800s. Before this, as early as the 1600s, condoms were made of materials such as sheepskins, goatskins, or bladders. The condom is still one of the most popular birth control devices, especially with the ability to make condoms out of superthin latex. Women as well as men carry condoms, to make sure that one is available when needed. The condom is the only form of birth control besides abstinence that also minimizes the transmission of sexually transmitted diseases.

A female version of the condom was introduced in the 1980s. Like the male condom, it helps protect against sexually transmitted diseases; however, it is slightly less effective at preventing pregnancy.

The Sponge

Remarkably, some techniques of birth control have not changed very much over time. More than three thousand years ago, Egyptian women used natural sponges to prevent sperm from fertilizing the egg. A far more effective modern counterpart is the contraceptive sponge. The sponge was removed from the market in 1994 due to concerns over toxic shock syndrome (TSS). TSS is a rare, but potentially fatal condition that first received attention because young women were leaving tampons in too long. However, the contraceptive sponge was reintroduced in 2003. The synthetic sponge contains a dose of spermicide to kill sperm before they can get to the cervix. The sponge has a dimple on one side for the cervix and a string on the other for easy removal. The sponge does not protect the user against sexually transmitted diseases. The failure rate for sponge users in the first year of use is about 16 percent. Sponges are also much less effective after childbirth, due to changes in the cervix.[15]

The Diaphragm

Latex diaphragms have not changed much since they were invented in the nineteenth century.[16] A similar device is the cervical cap, but this has not caught on in the United States since its invention also in the nineteenth century.[17] Both devices require a medical prescription. Both are coated with a spermicidal lubricant and inserted in the woman's vagina so that they cover the cervix. Using a diaphragm is like covering the cervix with an umbrella; it is awkward to manipulate and difficult to put in but covers far more area. Using a cervical cap is like covering the cervix with a ski cap. It fits more snugly and is much smaller, but requires a more intimate knowledge of the woman's anatomy.

Contraceptive Effectiveness Against Pregnancy and STDS[18]

Method	Theoretical Reliability	Actual Reliability	Failure Rate in First Year of Typical Use	Prescription Needed?	Protects Against STDs?
Abstinence	100%	?	?	No	Yes
No method	15%	15%	85%	No	No
Spermicide alone	94%	74%	26%	No	No
Female condom	95%	79%	21%	No	Yes
Cervical cap (and spermicide)	91%	80%	20%	Yes	No
Diaphragm (and spermicide)	94%	80%	20%	Yes	No
Withdrawal	96%	81%	19%	No	No
Natural Family Planning	98%	83–85%	15–17%	No	No
Contraceptive sponge	94%	84%	16%	No	No
Male condom	97%	85%	15%	No	Yes
Emergency contraception	97%	89%	11%	Yes (as of this writing)	No
Implants	99%	95%	5%	Yes	No
Pill	99%	95%	5%	Yes	No
Female sterilization (tubal ligation)	99%	99%	<1%	No, but requires surgery	No
IUD	99%	99%	<1%	Yes	No
Male sterilization (vasectomy)	99%	99%	<1%	No, but requires surgery	No

Natural Family Planning

Natural Family Planning is a method of preventing births that uses the woman's body signals. These signals are a combination of cervical mucus and basal body temperature—the woman's temperature taken before she moves at all in the morning. The calendar is also used in Natural Family Planning. Many people mistakenly refer to this as the "rhythm" method, which has gotten a lot of negative attention because of its unreliability. However, Natural Family Planning does require a committed, monogamous relationship. It also requires planning and organization, as well as a willingness to abstain from intercourse during the woman's fertile time, which may last for several days. It also does nothing to guard against STDs.

Abstinence

If done correctly, abstinence is 100 percent effective at preventing both pregnancy and STDs. However, many people who intend to be abstinent find that if they do not stick to their resolve, they have no backup method. Abstinence seems to be gaining in popularity. According to one poll conducted, 92 percent of teens say that being a virgin is generally a good thing.[19] However, according to *USA Today*, 99 percent of teens who don't pledge to be abstinent have sex before marriage—along with 88 percent of those who do pledge abstinence.[20] Perhaps being a virgin is generally perceived to be positive, but staying a virgin until marriage is a separate consideration. So it seems that many teens may say that abstinence is good, yet at the same time they have no plans to actually practice it.

Peter Bearman, Ph.D., from Columbia University's Department of Sociology, conducted the National Longitudinal Study of Adolescent Health. Bearman and his coauthor Hannah Brückner found that taking a pledge of abstinence has no significant effect on a person's chances of having a sexually

A young woman reads the results of a home pregnancy test. Thirteen percent of all births in the United States are to teenagers—three quarters of whom are unmarried.

transmitted infection. Teens who did not take the pledge often used contraceptives, which often also protect against STDs.

"It's difficult to simultaneously prepare for sex and say you're not going to have sex," Dr. Bearman says. "The message is really simple: 'Just say no' may work in the short term but doesn't work in the long term."[21] Bearman noted that part of the problem is that people who plan on abstinence do not have a backup plan for when Plan A fails.[22]

Emergency Contraception

Emergency contraception (EC) is sometimes called the morning-after pill. However, this is misleading, since it is not necessarily taken the morning after unprotected intercourse, but within seventy-two hours. It consists of hormones taken after unprotected intercourse in two doses twelve hours apart. EC is a combination of progestin and estrogen or progestin alone. Plan B is one brand of emergency contraception. EC works by stopping ovulation, fertilization, or implantation of the fertilized egg. However, if the embryo has become attached already, this pill will not cause the embryo to be expelled. EC will not work if the woman is already pregnant. This method is more effective the sooner it is taken.[23]

As of this writing, there is discussion of making emergency contraception available without a prescription, but that has not happened yet. People in favor of making it available over the counter (without a prescription) argue that having the pill more available would reduce the risk of unwanted pregnancies. People against making EC available over the counter argue that it would make people more likely to engage in unprotected sex.

Abortion

The word *abortion* means to stop something in progress. *Spontaneous abortion* is the technical term for miscarriage. When most people use the word *abortion*, they are referring to elective abortion, when means are taken to intentionally terminate a pregnancy.

Abortion is a hotly debated topic in the United States. Elective abortion became legal in the United States in 1973. Since then, many fewer women have died in illegal "back street" abortions, often performed in unsanitary conditions by people who were not doctors. Since the 1990s, abortion rates have declined, as have teenage birthrates and teenage pregnancy rates overall.[24]

There are two types of elective abortion: surgical and medical. Surgical abortions are performed in various ways depending on how far along a pregnancy is; they involve introducing a device or instrument into the uterus and removing the fetus. Medical abortions are performed by either an injection and pill or two types of pills. They cause the uterine lining to break down, ending the pregnancy, and then cause the uterus to contract and expel the fetus. A medical abortion can be performed up to sixty-three days after the last menstrual period.

Parenthood

Given a choice between hearing [a] daughter say "I'm pregnant" or "I used a condom," most mothers would get up in the middle of the night and buy them herself.
—M. Joycelyn Elders, M.D., U.S. surgeon general[25]

The highest rate for teenage births recorded in U.S. history was in 1957, when ninety-six out of one thousand young women aged fifteen to nineteen gave birth. Surprised? If you look beneath the surface, however, you see that the majority of teenage mothers from the 1950s to the 1970s were married. Some of the recent trends in teenage relationships are not surprising. After the 1970s, the majority of teenage mothers were unmarried. Teen birthrates in the mid-1980s were at a low point, at fifty to fifty-three births per thousand teenagers aged fifteen to nineteen.[26] In 2000, the rate dipped even lower, to less than fifty births per one thousand teenage girls. This trend holds true for teens of all races and ages.[27]

In discussing pregnancy and birthrates, it is important to note the difference between the two. Many pregnancies end in abortion or miscarriage. Many women, teenagers and adults, miscarry without knowing they were pregnant. Estimates vary widely, but a conservative guess is that about 20 percent of *known* pregnancies terminate on their own. Some experts estimate that 40 percent of all pregnancies end in miscarriage.[28]

Young women are still developing physically, emotionally, and intellectually. Many people report feeling in a state of flux until they hit their mid-twenties. Still, about 1 million American teens become pregnant each year, about 20,000 of them younger than fourteen.[29] In 1996, of the known 905,000 teenage pregnancies, 56 percent resulted in birth, 30 percent were intentionally aborted, and 14 percent ended in miscarriage.[30] Roughly the same percentages were found in 2000, of the known 841,450 pregnancies.[31] In the 2000s, 32 percent of young women who got pregnant before the age of twenty did not want to.[32] According to Myral Robbins of the American College of Osteopathic Physicians, "The majority of unplanned pregnancies occur within six months of first intercourse."[33]

Dangers of Early Childbearing

> *The teenage years are a time of personal discovery and fulfillment. They are not years well-suited to the nurturing of a future generation. We must make it possible for every teenager to prevent a pregnancy until that personal decision is a responsible and appropriate one and in the best interests of all involved.*
> —M. Joycelyn Elders, M.D., U.S. surgeon general[34]

Pregnant teenagers tend to seek less prenatal care than older women, thus jeopardizing not just the baby's health but their own. In addition, according to Adoption.com, "Babies born to teenagers are at risk for neglect and abuse because their young

Experts agree that teenage childbearing can cause physical, social, and emotional problems for both the mother and the baby.

mothers are uncertain about their roles and may be frustrated by the constant demands of caretaking."[35]

Many teenagers who marry soon have a second child. Unfortunately, teenagers who get married young and have children early also tend not to finish their schooling. As research has shown, without high school diplomas, people are often permanently stuck in low-paying jobs. About one third of teenage marriages will end in divorce within the first five years. After fifteen years, approximately half of those teenagers who got married when they were eighteen or nineteen will be divorced.[36]

Disease

Decades ago, descriptions of venereal diseases included syphilis, gonorrhea, and genital warts. Posters during World War II urged young military men to protect themselves. Abstinence and condom use became patriotic necessities. "Venereal disease helps the enemy," the posters proclaimed.[37]

In the 1960s, other diseases were identified as being risks of sexual contact, such as hepatitis. The term *sexually transmitted diseases*, or STDs, became more common than *venereal disease*. Another term for sexually transmitted disease is *sexually transmitted infection*, or STI.

In the early 1980s, a new plague was discovered—acquired immunodeficiency syndrome, or AIDS. This disease, which first emerged as a killer of young gay men and intravenous drug users, is caused by human immunodeficiency virus (HIV). Even young school children can easily name AIDS as a disease that can be spread by sexual contact. By the end of 2002, it was estimated that 42 million people worldwide were infected with HIV, the great majority in Third World countries. Some 25 million had died from AIDS.[38] According to the U.S. Centers for Disease Control and Prevention:

> Declines in AIDS deaths have slowed and the number of people living with AIDS has continued to grow. . . . AIDS incidence has . . . stabilized at roughly 40,000 diagnoses per year. . . . Further reductions in AIDS incidence and deaths will require improved access to and use of HIV testing, expanded access to care, and improvements in HIV therapies.[39]

Unfortunately, because of enormous amounts of publicity surrounding HIV and AIDS, teenagers sometimes overlook the dangers of other diseases. For example, human papillomavirus (HPV) has been shown to be one cause of cervical cancer. There are more than one hundred types of HP. Thirty of these are transmitted sexually and cause genital HPV. Exchange of bodily fluids is not necessary; only skin-to-skin contact. Condoms are not completely effective in preventing the spread of HPV.[40]

According to The Alan Guttmacher Institute, each year about one fourth of sexually active teenagers get a sexually transmitted disease.[41] If teens think they have an STD, they need to get help immediately.

Ignoring the problem will only make it worse. Continuing to have sexual relations is irresponsible and thoughtless. Beyond that, anyone who contracts an STD needs to tell any current and former sexual partners about it. Finally, teens need to make sure after they visit the doctor that they follow instructions for treatment.[42]

Common Signs/Symptoms of STDs

- Itching around the vagina and/or discharge from the vagina

- Discharge from the penis

- Pain during sex, when urinating, and/or in the pelvic area

- Sore throats in people who have oral sex

- Pain in the anus for people who have anal sex

- Painless red sores on the genital area, anus, tongue, and/or throat

- A scaly rash on the palms of your hands and the soles of your feet

- Dark urine; loose, light-colored stools; and yellow eyes and skin

- Small blisters that turn into scabs on the genital area

- Swollen glands, fever, and body aches

- Unusual infections, unexplained fatigue, night sweats, and weight loss

- Soft, flesh-colored warts around the genital area[43]

Sexual Assault

Girls face two major sexual issues in America in the 1990s: One is an old issue of coming to terms with their own sexuality, defining a sexual self, making sexual choices and learning to enjoy sex. The other issue concerns the dangers [that] girls face of being sexually assaulted. By late adolescence, most girls today either have been traumatized or know girls who have. They are fearful of males even as they are trying to develop intimate relations with them.

—Mary Pipher, U.S. clinical psychologist[44]

Young people face another risk from the secrecy surrounding sexual relationships. Often they do not realize that their relationship is not a healthy one. The American Psychological Association has created a Web site, "Love Doesn't Have to Hurt." In plain English, the Web site explains what teens have a right to expect from a relationship. Pain and shame are things they have a right to reject:

Every relationship has problems and upsets. That's just part of life. But if you see patterns of uncontrolled anger, jealousy, or possessiveness, or if there is shoving, slapping, forced sex, or other physical violence—even once—it's time to find help.[45]

Approximately one third of teens high school and college age encounter violence in an intimate relationship. More than half of all rapes are of young people, and most rapes are committed by an acquaintance of the victim. Unfortunately, teens often have fewer options for help than adults do.[46]

Rosalind Wiseman defines an abusive relationship as one in which "one person verbally, emotionally, financially, and physically (but not always) dominates, intimidates, and controls another."[47] It can be hard to recognize that you are in such a relationship, and it can be hard to get out of one. If you find yourself questioning whether you are in an abusive relationship, talk to your parents or a counselor to get their input and support.

Relationships that involve abuse—physical, emotional, or sexual—can be difficult to escape.

Economic Risks

One risk of sexual activity facing young people that is not discussed as often as STDs and pregnancy is economic risk. Studies have shown that among teenage girls who become pregnant, 17 percent become pregnant again within a year.[48] Teens who give birth often do not finish school and are then stuck in lower-paying jobs. Young men who become teenage fathers may seem to start out ahead, often because they are forced to earn money to support a family by dropping out of school. In their teens, they often earn more than their peers who are still in high school. However, when their peers graduate, teenage fathers soon lose that financial edge. They peak sooner and stay lower. Also, teenage parents often end up seeking public assistance and get into a financial trap they cannot get out of. Even if the couple does not get married, the father can be required to make paternity payments that continue until the child turns eighteen. If the couple is not married, the father has no rights to the child unless paternity is established through a blood test.

Internet Safety

As discussed earlier, many teens develop and maintain relationships over the Internet. Sometimes relationships can develop without people ever meeting face-to-face. There are several ways to interact with people on the Internet. The most secure is when kids chat with people they knew personally first before exchanging e-mail addresses or IM information. Similarly, people can do business online with stores and sellers they also visit in person. In this type of interaction, you want to be honest and accurate in your information.

Internet sites also have chat rooms and message boards. Many require that users be over eighteen years old. Kids need to make sure they are aware of the site's policies and get their parents' permission when required. (They could get their parents' permission even if the site does not require it, of course.) Teens who meet people first through chat rooms and message boards need to be cautious about how much information they reveal. Many reputable chat rooms advise that the kids identify themselves by first name only, and nothing else.

One way to avoid giving out your name or address online is to invent a character. Write down an entire "profile" and post it near your computer. Make up a name (first and last), address, phone number, ZIP code, age, school, and hobbies. Every time you are asked for such information, refer to your made-up character. Do not give out your real information. Making up a complete character profile, the way authors do, and printing it out will help you keep track of the person you say you are online.[49]

The Internet is also not as private as it might seem. There are public "shadows" left behind by exchanges between users. Teens need to be careful with what they send to other people in e-mails because it could be thought of as being obscene or threatening.

Experts say that you should never make arrangements to date anyone whom you have only met online. If someone asks you to get together, and you know him or her only through your online chats, discuss it with your parents first. People you "meet" on the Internet may not be representing themselves truthfully. That fifteen-year-old boy you've been chatting with for weeks might turn out to be a thirty-two-year-old man. Or that fourteen-year-old girl looking to hook up with somebody might be a sheriff looking for pedophiles.

How Adults Can Help Teens

Most parents want what is best for their children. Parents often want to help their teenagers make the right decisions. Unfortunately, what is right for the parents is not always what is right for the child. Rosalind Wiseman advises parents to focus their energies in six areas. (Her list was originally intended for parents of girls, but they apply to parents of boys as well):

1. Parents should teach their teens not to "blow off" their friends for a date.

2. Parents should help their teens create criteria for dating on their own terms and on their own timetables.

3. Parents should help their teens learn how to communicate clearly in intimate relationships.

4. Parents should help their teens respond to sexual harassment when flirting goes too far.

5. Parents should help their teens think about their readiness for sex. Are they ready to be responsible? Do they have the strength to say no if it is not what they want?

6. Parents should help their teens recognize when they are in an abusive relationship and know how to get out of it.[1]

I Love You, Leave Me Alone

Many teens act as if they wish their parents would go away, and vice versa. One teen, Stephen N. Dunay, is a staff writer for Sex Etc., a Web site run by teens for teens. In his article, "Parents Do Matter," Dunay points out teens' need for parents. "So, we push them aside and pretend that we can make it on our own, but who are we kidding?" he writes. "Our rebellious teen instinct tells us it's OK to love our parents, but not show it or act like we *need* them." Dunay points out that the need for parental guidance and supervision is important during many trials of the teenage years, but it is especially so "when it comes to sexual health issues." He cites polls that say that 45 percent of teens said that parents are the most influential people in their lives and that 88 percent of teens said that it would be easier to postpone sex if they could talk to their parents about it. "Don't put all the responsibility on [parents] to talk," Dunay says.[2]

Sex Education Starts at Home

Part of the job of parents is to educate the child on growing up, dating, and developing a healthy adult sexuality. Most parents are OK on the first two; it is the third one that causes many parents heartburn. One important thing that parents have realized through the years is that they cannot leave their children's sex

Parents are their children's first teachers. And though some adults feel that adolescents don't want to have anything to do with them, teens don't necessarily agree.

education solely to the schools. Most parents want to give their children their family's philosophy on sexual matters.

Gloria Feldt, former president of the Planned Parenthood Federation of America, has pointed out that the United States has the highest teenage pregnancy rate of the industrialized countries. "Is this because our kids are more sexually active?" she asks. "No. The difference is [that other countries have] defined the problem as 'teen pregnancy,' and we have allowed the problem to be 'teen sex.'"[3] The issues are related, of course. However, one is a health issue and the other is a values issue.

As with most things that parents want to teach their kids, their actions often speak louder than words. The words usually come in "the talk," where the parent sits down to explain the birds and the bees. Sometimes the talk never comes at all; the kids pick information up on their own from friends. Many times the talk is worthy of a medical-school presentation on anatomy and physiology. All the body parts are given labels and processes are explained. Then the overwhelmed kid is asked if he or she has any questions. What many parents leave out of the talk is the emotional part of sex. Douglass College student Shannon Rainey addressed this concern in an editorial in the student newspaper, *The Daily Targum.*

"It makes me wonder if we have lost touch with the romantic reasoning for this sexual behavior," Rainey writes. "I hope we have not become so inundated with the act itself that we have forgotten the emotion that should be behind it. If we forget love, can we truly realize the joy of physical contact?"[4]

Sex Education Continues at School

We learned in school about these steps in a relationship:

1. *Smile*

2. *Handshake*

3. *Hug*

4. *Peck, a little kiss on the cheek*

5. *Deep kiss*

6. *Exploring above the waist*

7. *Exploring below the waist*

8. *Sex*

In school they say you should stop at 4.5. I say you should stop at 7. Save 8 for marriage.
                    —Mark (who attends a private Catholic school)[5]

Sex education programs took off in the 1960s, primarily driven by health professionals. Since then, four types of programs have evolved. The first type focused on presenting facts about sexual intercourse and the problems of teenage pregnancy. The second type emphasized clarifying values, communicating, and decision making. The third type focused on abstinence to the extent that contraception was barely mentioned, except to point out that it often did not work. The last type combined the ideas of the previous three. This last approach seems to be the most effective, but many people are still advocating abstinence-only education.[6]

Abstinence-only sex education programs are heavily supported by the federal government. However, studies have not shown that abstinence-only programs are as successful as other approaches. Other programs acknowledge that some teens will still have intercourse. In that case, their approach is to make sure that teens make smart choices once they have chosen to engage in sexual activity.

A study was conducted by National Public Radio (NPR), the Kaiser Family Foundation, and the John F. Kennedy School of Government at Harvard University. It surveyed 1,759 Americans who were aged 18 or older. The survey showed that Americans support sex education in school overwhelmingly, with 93 percent in favor of it. However, only 15 percent of those polled want the abstinence-only approach taught in school.

When Cultures Collide

The United States has always been a country of immigrants, whether it is viewed as a "melting pot" (in which people adopted the customs of their new country and became more like one another) or a "salad bowl" (in which people retained more of their traditional ways and distinct characteristics). But for many people who come from other cultures, dating and relationships among American young people provide a real challenge. While parents want their children to make friends and be accepted, they do not want them to adopt behaviors they disapprove of. For example:

- In traditional Muslim families, women are expected to dress modestly, including wearing a head covering. Tank tops and low-cut jeans are definitely out. And during the month of Ramadan, the devout are expected to fast during the day—a practice that is not easy to follow on an American school schedule.

- Latin American girls do not usually date before their fifteenth birthday, an event celebrated by an elaborate party, the *quinceañera*. Even after that, dates are often chaperoned.

- Among Orthodox Jews, men and women who are not married to each other are not supposed to touch. And religious laws regarding food—*kasheruth*—can make it difficult to find an acceptable restaurant. So a school dance followed by a hamburger and shake at McDonald's is not on the agenda.

According to Charles L. Glenn of Boston University, "There's a tremendous fear (among immigrant parents) that kids will be sucked down by what they see as a tremendously destructive culture." And Benita Castro, a native of Mexico who now lives in Virginia, sums it up: "We are raising our kids in the United States, but we'll stick to our morals."[7]

Zeina, a young woman from a traditional family, tells her story:

I was in big trouble when my dad found out that I have a boyfriend. He took my car keys, my cell phone, I dunno what he did to my computer. I couldn't

When Cultures Collide *(continued)*

go to work or school; my father said he can care less. He was scared that I will call my boyfriend and I will see him at school or at work although I told him he doesn't live here. . . . I guess he didn't believe me. . . .

I am from Lebanon, a country in the Middle East. We have different religions in my country; it is not only Islam as most people think. Usually teenagers are not allowed to date regardless of their (religion). Dating is related to traditions and customs. But all teenagers date secretly. I used to date back home and nobody knew about him until I came here and I was crying and I had some type of depression. Most people do not want to see their daughters with a guy because they directly think about sex relations. Lebanese girls should be virgins till they (get) married. If you are not virgin and you got married, . . . when your husband finds out that you are not virgin he will divorce you at the same moment. Also, widows will typically never get married especially if they have some kids. Some of them do but they have to leave their children at their parents' house cause the (new) husband will not take care of them.

Nowadays everyone has boyfriend and girlfriend and live a love story and plan for marriage but everything should be done secretly. My mom knows about my boyfriend and she likes him but also she can't tell my father that she knows about him because she will be in trouble. She helps me a lot. My older brother used to have a girlfriend that my dad knew about but he was ok with that because he was a guy, nobody will know if he loses his virginity. . . . Also, in my country if you come from a rich family you have to marry a rich guy and vice versa. We still have arranged marriages, but the girl always has the right to refuse the guy. Nothing is obligatory. They believe that arranged marriages work better because they are based on logic and not driven by emotions that sometimes can hide a lot of problems about the partner.

All the girls date but nobody should know (about) it. The question that comes into my mind is, ok! so boys are allowed to date but girls are not. So (who) the boys are dating then?? It's funny.

I do not believe in sexual relations before marriage not because of my traditions, but because of my religion. I respect GOD and my religion. I am trying not to make any sins. Probably here it is easy for a guy to sleep with a girl but back home it is very hard. Also, the girls and boys do not leave their parents' home until they are done (with) education and get married.[8]

Nevertheless, 30 percent of the principals responding to the survey said that their schools taught abstinence only. More than one third of all the people answering the survey said that teens should be taught how to make responsible decisions about sex, not just how to abstain from it.[9]

Abstinence-only programs focus on abstaining from sexual relations. But how people define abstinence can vary. On one end of the continuum, abstinence can mean that neither person touches the other's genitals. This view would allow kissing but no heavy petting, no mutual masturbation, no oral sex or out-ercourse. And, of course, no intercourse. At the other end of the continuum, some people view abstinence as anything short of full penetration with orgasm. In the NPR/Kaiser/ Kennedy poll, 63 percent of the people polled believed that abstinence meant no intimate touching. Forty percent felt that abstinence meant no passionate kissing, and 44 percent thought it excluded masturbation, as well.[10]

Americans overwhelmingly support sex education in the schools, but only 15 percent believe in abstinence-only programs—the type endorsed by the federal government.

It is helpful to look at *why* abstinence is important. If absti- nence is considered a moral concern, then any type of sexual activity, such as flirting, kissing, or even hugging, might be thought of as immoral and therefore off limits. If abstinence is considered a practical concern, then abstinence might mean avoiding activities that could lead to contracting diseases or causing a pregnancy. In this view, intercourse, anal intercourse, and oral sex would be forbidden.[11]

Abstinence-only sex education programs are strongly promoted by evangelical religious groups. In the NPR/Kaiser/Kennedy poll discussed earlier, 81 percent of evangelical or born-again Christians said they believe that premarital sexual intercourse is

Sexuality education programs in schools have evolved in a number of different directions. Some stress "abstinence only," while others include a wider range of information, including methods of preventing pregnancy and STDs.

morally wrong. Similarly, 56 percent of the evangelical Christians said that schoolkids should not engage in passionate kissing, either.[12]

The Web site of the American College of Osteopathic Family Physicians says that the most effective programs are a combination of many factors. These factors include looking at values and norms, focusing on self-worth, developing interpersonal skills, recognizing family values, considering economic variables, and presenting facts on STDs, STD prevention, pregnancy, and contraceptives.[13]

Condoms in the Schools

Schools are beginning to provide condoms, either in the restrooms or through the nurse's office. When this concept was first introduced, arguments erupted. Many felt that access to birth control devices would encourage kids to have sexual intercourse. One controversial program in Massachusetts supplied condoms to high schools. When the policy was enacted in 1991, people feared that the presence of the condoms would increase teenagers' sexual activity. Research since then has shown that most of those fears were groundless. The frequency of intercourse did not increase for the group of students who were already engaged in sexual activity, nor did it encourage students who had not had sex previously to start. What the study did find, however, was that students in schools where condoms were available were twice as likely to use condoms as students in other schools and were less likely to use any other form of birth control. It is not clear if the presence of condoms in the schools had an effect on either rates of pregnancy or sexually transmitted diseases. The study concluded that pregnancy rates were the same for schools that provided condoms and for those that did not.[14]

You Know You Best

[As teenagers], the trauma of near-misses and almost-consequences usually brings us to our senses. We finally come down someplace between our parents' safety advice, which underestimates our ability, and our own unreasonable disregard for safety, which is our childlike wish for invulnerability. Our definition of acceptable risk becomes a product of our own experience.
    —Roger Gould, U.S. psychotherapist and author[15]

As a teenager, you receive information and opinions about sex, dating, and relationships from a number of different sources—family, friends, popular culture, school, religious groups, and others. Because our culture contains so many different points of view, the messages you receive inevitably conflict with each other. Different people have very different opinions about what is right, appropriate, or desirable.

As you mature, you will need to make decisions about what kind of behavior is right for you. The aim of this book has been to help you make those decisions responsibly.

When are you old enough to be able to decide for yourself? Somewhere in the middle of all the debate over "what's old enough?" you will find the answer that is right for you. Psychologist Linda Sonna says: "Having sexual intercourse involves sharing your body with someone else in the deepest, most intimate way possible, so it is like sharing your deepest, most important secret."[16]

With open eyes and an open heart, having a meaningful relationship can be one of the most fulfilling parts of life.

Chapter Notes

Chapter 1 Relationships: What's the Story?

1. Personal interview with LaRon (last name withheld), June 12, 2004.
2. E-mail from Sarah Heath to author, July 9, 2004.
3. Myral R. Robbins, DO, FACOFP, "Debate Over How to Reduce High Rate of Teen Pregnancy," *American College of Osteopathic Family Physicians*, n.d., <http://www.acofp.org/member_publications/camar_02.htm> (June 14, 2004).

Chapter 2 Communication

1. Instant messenger interview with Morgan (last name withheld), July 6, 2004.
2. Rosalind Wiseman, *Queen Bees and Wannabees: Helping Your Daughter Survive Cliques, Gossip, Boyfriends & Other Realities of Adolescence* (New York: Three Rivers Press, 2002), pp. 176, 179.
3. Dan Kindlon and Michael Thompson, *Raising Cain: Protecting the Emotional Life of Boys* (New York: Ballantine Books, 2000), p. 195.
4. Deborah Tannen, *You Just Don't Understand: Women and Men in Conversation* (New York: Quill, 2001), p. 85.
5. "Facts for Features," U.S. Census Bureau, September 24, 2003, <http://www.census.gov/Press-Release/www/releases/archives/facts_for_features/001369.html> (June 17, 2004).
6. Michael Pastore, "Internet Key to Communication Among Youth," January 25, 2002, <http://www.clickz.com/stats/sectors/demographics/print.php/5901_961881> (April 23, 2004).
7. Amy Bowles Reyer, "Generation IM," 2004, <http://tlc.discovery.com/convergence/teenspecies/articles/im.html> (June 17, 2004).
8. Ibid.
9. Ibid.
10. E-mail from Sarah Heath to author, July 9, 2004.

11. Dan Pankraz, "The Power of Teens Online," 2004, <http://www.brandchannel.com/papers_review.asp?sp_id=102> (June 17, 2002).

12. Ibid.

Chapter 3 Popularity and Body Image

1. Stedman Graham, *Move Without the Ball: Put Your Skills and Your Magic to Work for You!* (New York: Fireside/Simon & Schuster, 2004), p. 43.

2. Group interview with author, June 12, 2004.

3. Ibid.

4. "Body Image Timeline," *The Site.org*, 2004, <http://www.thesite.org/healthandwellbeing/mentalhealth/bodyimageandselfesteem/bodyimagetimeline> (January 16, 2006).

5. Etta Saltos, "Adapting the Food Guide Pyramid for Children: Defining the Target Audience," *Family Economics and Nutrition Review*, vol. 12, nos. 3, 4, 1999, <http://www.usda.gov/cnpp/FENR/fenrv12n4/fenrv12n4ps.pdf> (July 5, 2004).

6. Ibid.

7. "Teens' distorted body image may lead to unhealthy behaviours," *Women's Health Matters,* July 17, 2003, <http://www.womenshealthmatters.ca/news/news_show.cfm?number=266> (June 23, 2004).

8. Amy G. Miron and Charles D. Miron, *How to Talk With Teens About Love, Relationships, & S-E-X: A Guide for Parents* (Minneapolis: Free Spirit Publishing, Inc., 2002), pp. 120, 137.

9. Author's diaries from January 13, 1971, and January 13, 1972.

10. Dan Kindlon and Michael Thompson, *Raising Cain: Protecting the Emotional Life of Boys* (New York: Ballantine Books, 2000), p. 205.

11. Personal interview with Toni Cottongim, July 13, 2004.

12. E-mail from Michael Wilmington to author, March 27, 2004.

13. "Youth Prevention Curriculum: Full of Ourselves Project Description," *McLean Hospital*, n.d., <http://www.mclean.harvard. edu/education/youth/> (July 4, 2004).

14. Instant messenger interview with Morgan (last name withheld), July 6, 2004.

15. Linda Sonna, *The Everything Tween Book: A Parent's Guide to Surviving the Turbulent Preteen Years* (New York: Scholastic, 2003), p. 19.

16. Instant messenger interview with Morgan.

Chapter 4 Gender Identity and Sexual Orientation

1. Deborah Blum, "What's the Difference Between Boys and Girls?" *Life*, July 1999, p. 46.

2. John Colapinto, *As Nature Made Him: The Boy Who Was Raised as a Girl* (New York: Perennial/HarperCollins, 2001), p. 218.

3. Henk Asscheman, et al., "Definition and Synopsis of the Etiology of Adult Gender Identity Disorder and Transsexualism," *Gender Identity Research and Education Society*, n.d., <http://www. gires.org.uk/Web_Page_Assets/Etiology_definition_signed.htm> (July 24, 2004).

4. Barbara J. Heuberger, *Cultural Diversity: Building Skills for Awareness, Understanding and Application* (Dubuque: Kendall/Hunt, 2004), p. 57.

5. Michael Riera, *Uncommon Sense for Parents with Teenagers* (Toronto: Celestial Arts, 2004), p. 136.

6. Ann Heron, ed., *Two Teenagers in Twenty: Writings by Gay and Lesbian Youth* (New York: Alyson Books, 1994), p. 8.

7. Ibid., p. 161.

8. "The First Measured Century, Social Science in Americans' Bedroom: Alfred Kinsey Measures Sexual Behavior," Public Broadcasting System, n.d., <http://www.pbs.org/fmc/segments/ progseg10.htm> (October 21, 2005).

9. Lynda Madaras, with Area Madaras, *The "What's Happening to My Body?" Book for Girls: A Growing-Up Guide for Preteens and Teens,*

Including a Special Introduction for Parents (New York: Newmarket Press, 2000), p. 215.

10. Nicole Bengiveno, "Love That Dare Not Squeak Its Name," February 7, 2004; Larry Buhl, "Zoo drops efforts to turn penguins straight," *Gay Heroes.com: Gay & Lesbian People in History,* February 18, 2005, <http://www.gayheroes.com/penguins.htm> (March 12, 2005).

11. James Dobson, *Bringing Up Boys* (Wheaton, Ill.: Tyndale House Publishers, Inc., 2001), p. 115.

12. "The Body: Gay, Lesbian and Bisexual Issues," December 2000, <http://www.thebody.com/apa/apafacts.html> (March 13, 2005).

13. Ibid.

14. Personal interview with "Seth," November 18, 2003.

15. Heron, p. 68.

16. Leroy Aarons, *Prayers for Bobby: A Mother's Coming to Terms With the Suicide of Her Gay Son* (San Francisco: HarperSanFrancisco, 1995), p. 78.

17. "First came tears, fears; then resolve, activism," Parents, Families and Friends of Lesbians and Gays, n.d., <http://www.pflag.org/index.php?id=90> (September 20, 2005).

18. "The Coming Out Virtual Brochure" January 5, 2004, <http://www.usca.edu/cc/comingout.html> (June 19, 2004).

19. "The Hetrick-Martin Institute: The Past, Present and Future," 2002, <http://www.hmi.org/GeneralInfoAndDonations/AboutHMIAndHMHS/default.aspx> (March 13, 2005).

20. "About the Network," *Gay-Straight Alliance Network,* n.d., <http://www.gsanetwork.org/about/index.html> (October 21, 2005).

21. "Hypoactive Sexual Desire Disorder," *PsychNet-UK,* July 20, 2003, <http://www.psychnet-uk.com/dsm_iv/hypoactive_sexual_desire_disorder.htm> (March 15, 2005).

22. John Bonner, "Glad to Be Asexual," *NewScientist.com News Service,* March 10, 2005, <http://www.newscientist.com/article.ns?id=dn6533> (March 12, 2005).

Chapter 5   Special Relationships—When Boy Friends Become Boyfriends

1. Ericka Lutz, *The Complete Idiot's Guide to Friendship for Teens* (Indianapolis: Alpha/Pearson Education Company, 2001), ch. 9.

2. Melissa Glass, "How to Go From Crush to Couple: 7 Steps to Boyfriend Bliss," *Teen People*, June/July 2004, p. 154.

3. Rosalind Wiseman, *Queen Bees and Wannabees: Helping Your Daughter Survive Cliques, Gossip, Boyfriends & Other Realities of Adolescence* (New York: Three Rivers Press, 2002), p. 203.

4. Laurie Goodstein, "New Christian Take on the Old Dating Ritual," *The New York Times*, September 9, 2001.

5. Ibid.

6. "Ages for legal purposes: Age of simple majority," *Interpol*, February 6, 2003, <http://www.interpol.int/Public/Children/SexualAbuse/nationalLaws/csaUSA.asp> (June 19, 2004).

7. "Marriage Laws of the Fifty States, District of Columbia and Puerto Rico," *LII Legal Information Institute*, 1999, <http://www.law.cornell.edu/topics/Table_Marriage.htm> (February 15, 2006).

8. "Dating Around the World," *About.com*, n.d., <http://homeworktips.about.com/library/weekly/aa02001a.htm?iam=dpil&terms=%2Biran+%2> (October 22, 2005).

9. E-mail from Sarah Heath to author, July 9, 2004.

10. Ibid.

11. Ibid.

12. Ibid.

13. Lindsey MacAllister, "Change or Continuity? The Illinois Amish Wedding, 1880–1980," *Historia Online 2004*, <http://www.eiu.edu/~historia/2003/amish.htm> (September 16, 2005).

14. Ibid.

15. Lynda Madaras, with Area Madaras, *The "What's Happening to My Body?" Book for Girls: A Growing-Up Guide for Preteens and Teens, Including a Special Introduction for Parents* (New York: Newmarket Press, 2000), pp. 210–214.

16. Jennifer Augustine, Kayla Jackson, and Jane Norman, "Creating Inclusive Programs," *Advocates For Youth,* June 2002, <http://www.advocatesforyouth.org/publications/transitions/transitions1404_5.htm> (March 15, 2005).

17. Michael Riera, *Uncommon Sense for Parents With Teenagers* (Toronto: Celestial Arts, 2004), p. 121.

18. Heath.

19. Wiseman, p. 187.

20. Ibid., p. 230.

21. E-mails to author from Holly Chaker, May 7, 2004, and from Tuan Phan, April 24, 2004.

22. "Many Urban Teens With Boyfriends See Others," *OBGYN.net,* November 13, 2003, <http://www.obgyn.net/newsheadlines/womens_health-Adolescent_Sexuality-20031113-0.asp> (June 19, 2004).

23. Ray Dudley, "The ABCD of LGBT Dating," *teenwire.com,* February 20, 2003, <http://www.teenwire.com/infocus/2003/if-20030220p207-dating.php> (June 19, 2004).

24. "The Coming Out Virtual Brochure," January 5, 2004, <http://www.usca.edu/cc/comingout.html> (June 19, 2004).

Chapter 6   Sexual Intercourse and Other Zones
of Controversy

1. Instant messenger interview with Morgan (last name withheld), July 6, 2004.

2. Linda Sonna, *The Everything Tween Book: A Parent's Guide to Surviving the Turbulent Preteen Years* (New York: Scholastic, 2003), p. 228.

3. Subhash Rao, "Hepatitis B," *Laksh-Deep Hospital & ICCU,* n.d., <http://www.lakshdeep.com/hepatitisb.htm> (March 15, 2005).

4. Sonna, pp. 226–227.

5. Barbara Coloroso, *Kids Are Worth It,* ch. 14, 1994, <http://www.bartleby.com/66/39/13039.html> (June 23, 2004).

6. Stedman Graham, *Move Without the Ball: Put Your Skills and Your Magic to Work for You!* (New York: Fireside/Simon & Schuster, 2004), p. 124.

7. Nina Bernstein, "Behind Fall in Pregnancy, a New Teenage Culture of Restraint," *The New York Times*, March 7, 2004, p. 1.

8. Melissa Daly, "The New Double Standard," *Seventeen*, January 2003, p. 113.

9. Anna Mulrine, "Risky Business," *U.S. News and World Report*, May 27, 2002, p. 46.

10. Lorraine Ali and Julie Scelfo, "Choosing Virginity," *Newsweek*, December 9, 2002, p. 62.

11. Lisa Remez, "Special Report: Oral Sex Among Adolescents: Is It Sex or Is It Abstinence?" *Family Planning Perspectives*, vol. 32, no. 6, November/December 2000, p. 4.

12. Daly, p. 114.

13. *Today Show*, NBC, October 21, 2005.

14. "Birth Control Pill," *TeensHealth*, April 2003, <http://kidshealth.org/teen/sexual_health/contraception/contraception_birth.html> (March 15, 2005).

15. "Overview: Birth Control," *American Pregnancy Association*, 2003, <http://wwww.americanpregnancy.org/preventingpregnancy/birthcontrolfailure.html> (January 16, 2006).

16. "The Birth of Contraception," *By Girls for Girls: A Project by and for Adolescent Girls*, 2003, <http://bygirlsforgirls.org/bg4g2003/contraception.html> (February 16, 2006).

17. Ibid.

18. Information compiled from Monnica T. Williams, "Understanding Your Risks: Effective Contraception," *Contraceptive Information Resource*, n.d., <http://www.contracept.info/risks.php> (February 16, 2006), and Cynthia Haines, ed., "Sexual Health: Your Guide to Birth Control," *WebMD*, February 2005, <http://www.webmd.com/content/article/45/2953_483.htm?z=2953_00000_0000_rl_06#7> (January 16, 2006).

19. Daly, p. 113.

20. "Study: Abstinence pledges not reducing rates of STDs,"
    USATODAY.com, March 9, 2004. <http://www.usatoday.com/
    news/health/2004-03-09-abstinence-study_x.htm> (July 25, 2004).

21. Ibid.

22. Bernstein, p. 36.

23. "Emergency Contraception," *National Women's Health Information
    Center*, n.d., <http://www.women4women.gov/faq/
    econtracep.htm> (October 21, 2005).

24. Patricia Donovan, "Falling Teen Pregnancy, Birthrates: What's
    Behind the Declines?" *Alan Guttmacher Institute*, October 1998,
    <http://www.guttmacher.org/pubs/journals/gr010506.html>
    (April 23, 2004).

25. Joyceleyn Elders, Testimony before the U.S. Senate's Labor and
    Human Resources Committee, *The New York Times*, July 24, 1993,
    p. 6, <http://www.bartleby.com/66/26/18626.html> (June 23,
    2004).

26. National Center for Health Statistics, press release, April 30, 1998,
    <http://www.hhs.gov/news/press/1998pres/980430.html> (June 23,
    2004).

27. Heather Boonstra, "Teen Pregnancy: Trends and Lessons Learned,"
    Alan Guttmacher Institute, February 2002. <http://www.
    guttmacher.org/pubs/tgr/05/1/gr050107.html> (September 24,
    2004).

28. "Miscarriage," University of California at Santa Barbara, *Sex Info*,
    n.d., <http://www.soc.ucsb.edu/sexinfo/
    ?article=pregnancy&refid=011> (March 15, 2005).

29. Alan Guttmacher Institute, "U.S. Teenage Pregnancy Statistics with
    Comparative Statistics for Women Aged 20–24," February 19,
    2004, <http://www.agi-usa.org/pubs/teen_stats.html> (January 16,
    2006).

30. Alan Guttmacher Institute, "Teen Sex and Pregnancy," September
    1999, <http://www.agi-usa.org/pubs/fb_teen_sex.html>
    (September 28, 2004).

31. Alan Guttmacher Institute, "U.S. Teenage Pregnancy Statistics with
    Comparative Statistics for Women Aged 20–24," February 19,

2004, <http://www.agi-usa.org/pubs/teen_stats.html>
(September 28, 2004).

32. Daly, p. 115.

33. Myral R. Robbins, DO, FACOFP, "Debate Over How to Reduce High Rate of Teen Pregnancy," *American College of Osteopathic Physicians*, n.d., <http://www.acofp.org/member_publications/camar_02.htm> (June 14, 2004).

34. U.S. Department of Health and Human Services, "Special Focus: Surveillance for Reproductive Health," *Morbidity and Mortality Weekly Report*, CDC Surveillance Summaries. Atlanta, 1993, p. v.

35. "When Children Have Children," *adoption.com*, 2004, <http://library.adoption.com/Teenage-Pregnancy/When-Children-Have-Children> (June 15, 2004).

36. Naomi Seiler, "Is Teen Marriage a Solution?" Center for Law and Social Policy, April 2002, p. 7.

37. "Venereal Disease," *National Library of Medicine*, September 26, 2003, <http://www.nlm.nih.gov/exhibition/visualculture/venereal.html> (June 23, 2004).

38. "AIDS Marches On," *Vision Foundation for a New World*, 2002, <http://www.vision.org/trdl/2002/trdl021202.html> (March 15, 2005).

39. "Update: AIDS—United States, 2000," *Centers for Disease Control and Prevention*, July 11, 2002, <http://www.ced.gov/od/oc/media/mmwrnews/n020712.htm> (January 16, 2006).

40. "Learn about HPV," *American Social Health Association*, 2005, <http://www.ashastd.org/hpv/hpv_learn_fastfacts.cfm> (October 22, 2005).

41. Alan Guttmacher Institute, "Teen Sex and Pregnancy."

42. "Sexually Transmitted Diseases (STDs)," *Cincinnati Children's Hospital*, June 1999, <http://www.cincinnatichildrens.org/health/info/teen/diagnose/stds.htm> (November 1, 2005).

43. "STDs: Common Symptoms & Tips on Prevention," *Familydoctor.org*, April 2004, <http://familydoctor.org/165.xml> (March 15, 2005).

44. Mary Pipher, *Reviving Ophelia: Saving the Selves of Adolescent Girls* (New York: Ballantine Books, 1994), p. 244.

45. "Love Shouldn't Hurt Like This!" American Psychological Association, <http://apa.org/pi/pii/teen/teen2.html> (March 18, 2004).

46. "Safe Horizon Current Issues: Teen Relationship Abuse," *Safe Horizon*, 2000, <http://www.dvsheltertour.org/teen.html> (March 18, 2004).

47. Rosalind Wiseman, *Queen Bees and Wannabees: Helping Your Daughter Survive Cliques, Gossip, Boyfriends & Other Realities of Adolescence* (New York: Three Rivers Press, 2002), p. 269.

48. Robbins.

49. Sonna, p. 217.

Chapter 7   How Adults Can Help Teens

1. Rosalind Wiseman, *Queen Bees and Wannabees: Helping Your Daughter Survive Cliques, Gossip, Boyfriends & Other Realities of Adolescence* (New York: Three Rivers Press, 2002), pp. 260–261.

2. Stephen N. Dunay, "Parents Do Matter," *Sex Etc.*, April 15, 2004, <http://www.sxetc.org/index.php?topic=Stories&sub_topic=Sex&content_id=3150> (April 22, 2004).

3. Myral R. Robbins, DO, FACOFP, "Debate Over How to Reduce High Rate of Teen Pregnancy," *American College of Osteopathic Family Physicians,* n.d., <http://www.acofp.org/member_publications/camar_02.htm> (June 14, 2004).

4. Shannon Rainey, "The Birds and the Bees," *The Daily Targum*, November 5, 2002, <http://www.dailytargum.com/news/2002/11/05/Opinions/Birds.And.The.Bees-314792.shtml> (March 14, 2005).

5. Personal interview with Mark (last name withheld), June 2004.

6. Robbins.

7. Mary Ann Zehr, "Culture Clash," *Education Week*, February 5, 2003, pp. 26–30.

8. Email from Zeina (last name withheld) to author, May 20, 2004.

9. National Public Radio, "Sex Education in America," February 24, 2004, <http://www.npr.org/templates/story/story.php?storyID=1622610> (September 28, 2004).

10. Ibid.

11. Charlotte Schramm, "What does it mean to teach abstinence?" *Education*, Summer 1996, <http://www.findarticles.com/p/articles/mi_qa3673/is_199607/ai_n8743413> (March 14, 2005).

12. National Public Radio.

13. Robbins.

14. Adam Marcus, "Condoms in Schools Don't Promote Sex," *Health On the Net Foundation*, May 28, 2003. <http://www.hon.ch/News/HSN/513347.html> (July 24, 2004).

15. Roger Gould, *Transformations,* sec. 2, ch. 3, 1978, <http://www.bartleby.com/66/13/25713.html> (June 23, 2004).

16. Linda Sonna, *The Everything Tween Book: A Parent's Guide to Surviving the Turbulent Preteen Years* (New York: Scholastic, 2003), pp. 226–227.

Glossary

abortion—The ending of a pregnancy. Spontaneous abortion is the technical term for miscarriage. Elective abortion refers to intentionally terminating a pregnancy.

abstinence—Refraining from having sex. Sometimes used to refer to any intimate contact.

age of consent—The age at which a person is considered mature enough to be able to consent on his or her own to sexual relations.

asexual—Not experiencing sexual attraction, or not feeling compelled to act upon any sexual attraction one might feel.

bisexual—Attracted to people of both sexes.

celibacy—The state of not having sex.

cervical cap—A small latex contraceptive device, available by medical prescription only, that is coated with spermicide and fits snugly onto a woman's cervix.

come out—To identify oneself as gay.

condom—A contraceptive device, usually made out of latex, that fits over the penis and prevents sperm from entering the vagina.

contraceptives—Methods used to prevent pregnancy.

contraceptive sponge—A contraceptive device inserted into the vagina that contains a dose of spermicide to kill sperm before they can get to the cervix.

diaphragm—A latex contraceptive device, available by medical prescription only, that is coated with spermicide and inserted in the vagina so that it covers the cervix.

gender identity—How a person sees himself or herself, as masculine or feminine.

gender reassignment—A long, involved, and expensive process to change one's body from the gender it appears to be to the gender with which the person identifies.

heterosexual—Attracted to the opposite sex. Another term for heterosexual is straight.

homosexual—Attracted to the same sex. Another term for homosexual is gay.

intersexual (formerly hermaphrodite)—A person whose gender is not clear at birth.

lesbian—A woman who is attracted to other women.

LGBTQ—Lesbian, gay, bisexual, transgendered/transsexual, or queer/questioning.

Natural Family Planning (NFP)—A method of preventing pregnancy that uses the woman's body signals, such as cervical mucus and body temperature, to determine whether it is a good time to have sex without conceiving.

outercourse—Sexual activity without anal or vaginal penetration.

puberty—The time during which adolescents become physically capable of sexual reproduction.

sexual orientation—Whether one is attracted to one's own sex or to the opposite sex.

STD or STI—Sexually transmitted disease/sexually transmitted infection.

transgender—Having a gender identity that differs from the body one was born with.

transnatural—One who identifies with the opposite gender but has decided not to have genital surgery.

transsexual—One who identifies with the opposite gender.

virgin—A person who has not had sexual relations with another person.

Further Reading

Books

Brynie, Faith Hickman. *101 Questions About Sex and Sexuality— With Answers for the Curious, Cautious, and Confused.* Brookfield, Conn.: Twenty-First Century Books, 2003.

Fox, Annie. *Can You Relate? Real-World Advice for Teens on Guys, Girls, Growing Up, and Getting Along.* Minneapolis, Minn.: Free Spirit Publishing, 2000.

Madaras, Lynda, with Area Madaras. *The "What's Happening to My Body?" Book for Boys: A Growing-Up Guide for Preteens and Teens, Including a Special Introduction for Parents.* New York: NewMarket Press, 2000.

————. *The "What's Happening to My Body?" Book for Girls: A Growing-Up Guide for Preteens and Teens, Including a Special Introduction for Parents.* New York: NewMarket Press, 2000.

Marcus, Eric. *What If Someone I Know Is Gay? Answers to Questions About Gay and Lesbian People.* New York: Price Stern Sloan, 2000.

Peacock, Judith. *Dating and Sex: Defining and Setting Boundaries.* Mankato, Minn.: LifeMatters, 2001.

Internet Addresses

Sexuality Information and Education Council of the United States (SIECUS)
<http://www.siecus.org/pubs/fact/fact0007.html>

Teenagers Today site for teens from iParenting.com
<http://www.teenagerstoday.com>

TeenWire for information about sexuality and relationships from Planned Parenthood
<http://www.teenwire.com>

Index